An Apple a Day

Edited by: Shirley F. Burd
Cheryl C. Stegbauer
Linda S. White

**Published by
District #1
Tennessee Nurses' Association
Memphis, Tennessee
1981**

District #1
Tennessee Nurses' Association
Post Office Box 40801
Memphis,TN 38104

First Printing   1981   5,000

International Standard Book Number—0-939114-32-1

Printed in the United States of America
Wimmer Brothers Fine Printing & Lithography
Memphis, Tennessee 38118
"Cookbooks of Distinction" ™

Cookbook Committee

Chairman

Tine Keller

Illustrations

Patti Scott

Patricia D. Hallmark

Barbara Manning

Patricia Meade

Joyce Montgomery

Kay Morton

Jo Pool

Linda S. White

Pat Worley

Martha C. Yancey

Thanks also to Emma Clayborne, R.D.; Carolyn Foster, R.D.; Ken Hagenback, Wimmer Brothers; Dickie Stafford, Wimmer Brothers; Shirley Johnston; Mary Beth Murphy; Bobby G. Redmond, R.D.; Kathy Schultz, R.D.; Brenda Speight, R.D.; and Pat Worley.

President's Statement

An Apple a Day shares with you the heritage of our profession, our homes, and our restaurants. The promotion of health through good nutrition has been a tenet of nursing since at least, Florence Nightingale. The promotion of good eating is a national tradition, highly endorsed by this region and the Memphis area. This cookbook combines our interests in the preparation of food with nursing's age-old concern, the promotion of health through good nutrition.

The initial section shares with you some of the fare of our Memphis area restaurants. We assure you that these delights are but a sampling of the good eating available in the great restaurants of our Memphis area. Section II shares with you some of the hospitality and heritage of our homes. While all these recipes are used in our own Memphis area homes, some come from other states and their "true owners" have permitted us to include them in our book. The final section provides some nutritional information of importance to all of us. Herein, you'll find helpful tips on maintaining health.

We thank our colleagues, friends, relatives and local restaurateurs for their enthusiastic support of this venture in sharing our heritage with you. So—use An Apple a Day and enjoy it as much as the many members of our organization have enjoyed its preparation!

Shirley F. Burd
President, District #1,
Tennessee Nurses' Association

Table of Contents

District #1, Tennessee Nurses' Association has no reason to doubt that recipe ingredients, instructions, and directions will work successfully. However, the ingredients, instructions and directions have not necessarily been thoroughly or systematically tested, and the cook should not hesitate to test and question procedures and directions before preparation. The recipes in this book have been collected from various sources, and neither District #1, Tennessee Nurses' Association, nor any contributor, publisher, printer, distributor or seller of this book is responsible for errors or omissions.

District #1, Tennessee Nurses' Association extends its appreciation to all members, friends, consultants and restaurants who contributed to this book, edited the recipes, and typed the rough drafts. Regretably, not all material submitted could be used in this volume due to space. We particularly acknowledge the contributions of our typists, Betty B. Barnes, Linda Pratt and Carolyn M. Oxford.

Tine Keller, Chairman
Cookbook Committee

I. Memphis Area Restaurants...

*Shirley F. Burd and
Linda S. White, Eds.*

CREAM OF PIMIENTO

12 ounces onion, chopped
6 ounces butter
16 ounces pimiento, chopped
6 ounces flour
1½ quarts milk
1½ pints cream, whipped
1½ quarts chicken stock

4½ cups cheddar cheese, grated
1 tablespoon salt
¼ tablespoon white pepper
1 tablespoon Worcestershire sauce
Parsley sprigs

Sauté onions in butter until soft but not brown. Add pimiento and heat for 2 minutes. Blend in the flour. Mix in mix, cream and stock. Continue heating until soup has thickened. *DO NOT BOIL!!* Add cheese and stir until melted and smooth. Add seasonings. Remove from heat. Garnish servings with parsley.

Larry Stafford
#1 Beale Street
Memphis,TN

1 BEALE ST.
Bar and Restaurant

Entertainment Nightly
Greatest Steaks and Burgers
Award Winning Happy Hour

BLOODY MARY MIX

2 (1 quart 14 ounce) cans V-8 juice
2 (10½ ounce) cans beef broth
7-10 shakes Worcestershire sauce
15 shakes salt
20 shakes pepper
15 shakes celery salt
8 dashes hot pepper sauce
4 dashes bitters
1-1½ ounces lime juice

Pour all ingredients into a gallon container. Shake well. Mix with vodka and garnish with a squeeze of lime and a stalk of celery.

Note: We find a gallon plastic milk container works well because one can replace the cap and shake vigorously.

Ken Truman
Bombay Bicycle Club—Overton Square
2120 Madison Avenue
Memphis, TN

Bombay Bicycle Club
A COOKERY AND SALOON
IN OVERTON SQUARE

CREAM OF ASPARAGUS SOUP

½ bunch of scallions, chopped
2 pounds canned asparagus
  spears
3 tablespoons butter
3 tablespoons flour

1 cup chicken stock, warm
1 quart half and half
salt to taste
white pepper to taste

Sauté scallions in butter until tender. At last minute add asparagus to heat. Remove vegetables and puree in food processor. Set aside. Make roux by melting butter in sauce pan and adding flour. Stir until lightly brown. Add warm chicken stock and stir until mixture is blended to a smooth consistency. Lower heat and add the half and half. Continue to cook until mixture thickens to desired consistency. Remove from heat and add the pureed vegetables. Add salt and pepper to taste. If the soup is too thick, add more half and half.

Ken Truman
Bombay Bicycle Club—Overton Square
2120 Madison Avenue
Memphis, TN

Bombay Bicycle Club

A COOKERY AND SALOON
IN OVERTON SQUARE

DRESSING

1 onion
1 green pepper
3 celery stalks
1 quart (approximately) chicken
 or turkey broth
salt and black pepper to taste

2 skillets of milk cornbread,
 baked, cooled, crumbled
1 tablespoon sage
1 tablespoon poultry seasoning
8 eggs

Chop finely onion, green pepper, and celery and boil in broth until tender. Add all other ingredients. Preheat oven to 350 degrees. Bake in greased 9x12 inch baking dish 35 minutes. Serve with gravy and top with chopped hard boiled egg. Serves 12.

Milton Wiggens
Buntyns Restaurant
3070 Southern
Memphis, TN

CHILLED STRAWBERRY SOUP

1 pint strawberries
1 cup sour cream
1 pint half and half cream
1 pint whole milk

1 ounce lemon juice
6 ounces strawberry liquor
(red food coloring optional)

Puree one half of the cleaned strawberries in an electric blender until smooth. Thinly slice the remaining berries and keep aside. Combine all ingredients other than sliced strawberries. Blend until smooth and of a creamy consistency. Add sliced strawberries and chill for 6-8 hours. Serve in chilled bowl or glass with whole strawberry or mint garnish:

Chef Robert Sternburgh
Dr. J. T. Jabbour
The Carriage House
680 Adams-Rear
Memphis, TN

SPINACH PIE (SPANAKOPETA)

2 pounds fresh spinach
1 bunch green scallions
1 pound Greek feta cheese
7 whole extra large eggs

salt, to taste
white pepper, to taste
1 pound butter, melted, divided
1 pound filo pastry sheets

Wash spinach, squeezing out excess moisture and drain on paper toweling. Cut off coarse stems as you wash it. Tear drained spinach into pieces and place in large bowl. Chop scallions and add to spinach. Add crumbled cheese, *unbeaten eggs,* and season to taste with salt and white pepper. Pour two sticks of melted butter over this mixture and toss lightly to combine ingredients. Place six to eight pastry sheets in 10x15 pan, greasing pan well with pastry brush dipped in melted butter and brushing each filo sheet with melted butter as it is placed in the pan. Place spinach mixture in pan being careful not to add any watery mixture that may have accumulated in the bottom of the bowl. Cover with six individually buttered pastry sheets. Neaten edges by rolling the bottom sheets over the top sheets of pastry. Preheat oven to 350 degrees. Cut lengthwise through *top* of pastry sheets about every 3½ inches, as illustrated.

This will assure a crisp and not soggy pastry. Bake for one hour. Cool slightly and make vertical cuts to form squares. This may be frozen in pan before baking, or it may be frozen in individual portions after baking. Polyunsaturated margarine may be substituted for butter for those on a restrictive diet. Serves 24.

Harry Harris
Claybrook Restaurant
220 So. Claybrook
Memphis, TN

POTATO ROLLS

1 package instant mashed
  potatoes (4 serving size)
1 package active dry yeast
4½-4¾ cups all purpose flour

½ cup shortening
½ cup sugar
1 teaspoon salt
2 eggs, beaten

Prepare potatoes according to package directions: use any brand that *does not* call for milk as the fluid. In a large bowl, stir together 2 cups of the flour with the yeast. Mix together the shortening, sugar and salt and then, add the potatoes: combine with the flour and yeast. Mix in the remaining flour to make a soft dough. Cover and refrigerate several hours, or use as needed. Shape into rolls and place in greased pans. Let them rise. Preheat to 375 degrees. Bake 25-30 minutes.

Charles and Jean Thomsa
Conestoga Steaks
1397 Central Avenue
Memphis, TN

CONESTOGA STEAKS

FLATBOAT GUMBO

¼ cup bacon grease
2 tablespoons flour
4 large onions, coarsely
  chopped
½ cup smoked ham, cubed
2 gallons water, divided
3 pounds okra, sliced
6 cloves garlic
1½ teaspoons thyme
4 bay leaves

2 quarts canned tomatoes,
  mashed fine
1½ teaspoons black pepper
1½ teaspoons red pepper
1 tablespoon salt
5 pounds crab meat (optional)
7½ pounds shrimp, small
  (200 to the pound)
1½ tablespoons gumbo filé
1 tablespoon parsley flakes

Brown flour in bacon grease. Add onions and ham. Cook until light brown. Add ½ gallon water and remaining ingredients except for the shrimp, parsley and filé. Simmer 15 minutes. Add the remaining water. Boil for 1½ hours. Add shrimp 30 minutes before serving. Add parsley just before serving. Add gumbo filé slowly while stirring.

Frank and Mary Taylor
Doebler's Dock
110 Wagner Pl.
Memphis, TN

Doebler's Dock

LAVOSH
(Armenian Cracker Bread)

¾ cup water, warm
1 package active dry yeast
¼ teaspoon salt
½ teaspoon sugar
1 egg beaten with 1-2
tablespoons water

2½ cups flour or 1 cup whole
wheat flour and 1½ cups
white flour
celery salt
sesame seeds

Dissolve yeast in the warm water. Add salt, sugar, egg and flour. Knead until smooth, adding a small amount of flour if dough is too sticky. In a covered greased bowl, let rise again until double, about 2 hours. Punch down. Let rise again until double in bulk, about 1 hour. (The second rise may be done in the refrigerator. Refrigerate 4 hours or overnight.) Divide dough into 6 pieces. Roll out to ¹⁄₁₆ inch. It may be easier to roll out, wait, and then finish rolling. Put each cracker on a cookie sheet. Preheat oven to 350 degrees. Brush with beaten egg and water. Sprinkle with celery salt and sesame seeds. Bake until brown, about 10 minutes.

Martha Brahm
Fascinating Foods Catering Service
426 South Highland
Memphis, TN

FASCINATING FOODS

PAUL ZILCH
MARTHA LEE
BRAHM

TROUT MARGUERY

28 ounces boneless trout
4 tablespoons onlons, chopped
8 ounces white wine
2 cups water
1 teaspoon salt
dash of pepper, to taste

4 ounces butter
4 shrimp, split in half
12 mushrooms
2 tablespoons flour
6 ounces Hollandaise Sauce

Season fish, poach 5 to 6 minutes in a pan with the onions, wine, water, salt and pepper. Lift the fish carefully into a casserole dish. Strain the liquid and set aside. Heat the butter in the pan, add shrimp, and brown in butter. Add the mushrooms, brown 5 minutes. Place shrimp and mushrooms on fish. Put flour in pan, simmer 5 minutes but do not brown. Add the reserved liquid and whip smooth. Add Hollandaise Sauce to pan. Whip smooth. Pour sauce over fish, shrimp and mushrooms. Glaze under the broiler. Garnish with lemon and sprinkle with chopped parsley. Serves 4.

John Fields
Four Flames Restaurant
1085 Poplar Avenue
Memphis, TN

FOUR FLAMES

"FRIDAY'S HOT-DANG CHILI"

30 pounds ground beef
5 large onions, chopped
3 bell peppers, chopped
2 #10 cans tomatoes
2 #10 cans chili
2 #10 cans tomato puree
¼ cup cumin

2 tablespoons red pepper
2 tablespoons white pepper
1 tablespoon garlic powder
½ box salt
1 lb. chili powder
Tabasco—to taste

Cook beef, onions and peppers until ground beef is browned, breaking up meat with a paddle. Remove as much grease as possible. Add the remaining ingredients. Chili should be cooled to room temperature, then kept in the walk-in refrigerator until needed. Yield: approximately 4 gallons.

Note: This can be cut in half if you do not wish to make the entire 4 gallons. However, this recipe freezes very well.

David A. Broyles
Friday's
2115 Madison Avenue
Memphis, TN

MEMPHIS' FAVORITE GATHERING PLACE
"WHERE IT ALL BEGAN"
IN
OVERTON SQUARE

SPINACH AND EGGS GRISANTI

1 package (10 ounces) frozen
   spinach, chopped
2 slices bacon
3 tablespoons olive oil
1 small clove garlic, minced
¼ teaspoon salt
⅛ teaspoon pepper

¼ teaspoon monosodium
   glutamate
1 tablespoon Parmesan cheese,
   grated
2 eggs
2 tablespoons Parmesan
   cheese, grated

Cook frozen spinach according to package directions. Drain thoroughly, pressing out as much fluid as possible. Sauté bacon until crisp. Drain on a paper towel. In a skillet, heat the olive oil and add the garlic. Cook until golden brown. Add the spinach, salt, pepper and monosodium glutamate. Mix. Spread the mixture over the bottom of the skillet and sprinkle with' cheese. Cook turning spinach over until it is very hot. Break in the eggs and keep on turning the spinach until eggs are cooked. Crumble and add the bacon. Stir to mix well. Drain off any excess oil. Serve on a warm serving platter. Sprinkle with Parmesan cheese. Serve with brioche or hot popovers. Serves 2.

John Anthony Grisanti
Grisanti's Restaurants, Inc.
1489 Airways Blvd.
Memphis, TN

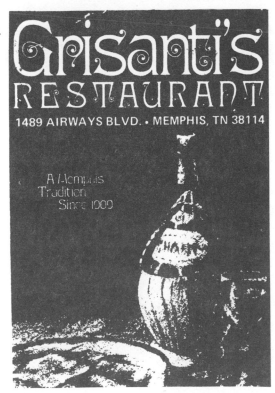

17

MOUSSAKA

1½ pounds ground beef
1 onion, chopped
1 clove garlic, finely cut
½ stick butter (¼ cup)
1½ teaspoons salt
¼ teaspoon pepper
¼ cup fresh parsley, chopped

¼ teaspoon cinnamon
1 (8 ounce) can tomato sauce
1 cup water
2 large eggplants
¼ cup Romano or Parmesan
   cheese, grated

Brown meat with onion, garlic, butter, salt and pepper. Skim fat off. Add parsley, cinnamon, tomato sauce and water. Simmer until it thickens, about 30 minutes. Slice eggplant lengthwise. Soak 15 minutes in salted water. Drain thoroughly and pat dry with towel. Fry each slice in hot vegetable oil until lightly brown, draining on paper towels. Alternate layers of sliced eggplant, cheese and meat in that order in a 11x17-inch baking dish, ending with eggplant on top sprinkled with cheese. Spread crema sauce over top. Preheat oven to 350 degrees. Bake for 45 minutes until top is golden brown.

Crema Sauce:
6 tablespoons butter
4 tablespoons flour
3 cups milk
6 egg yolks, beaten

¼ cup Romano or Parmesan
   cheese, grated
salt to taste
pepper to taste

Make roux with butter and flour, stirring constántly. Add milk gradually, stirring 'til thickened. *Slowly* add egg yolks, cheese, salt and pepper. Cook about 10 minutes until mixture begins to thicken.

C. B. Taras
Jim's Place East
5560 Shelby Oaks Drive
Memphis, TN

JIM'S PLACE EAST

SAUCE VINAIGRETTE

1 tablespoon wine vinegar
1 tablespoon lemon juice
salt and pepper, to taste

¼ teaspoon dry mustard
8 tablespoons French olive oil
½ tablespoon minced shallots

Mix vinegar, lemon juice, salt, pepper and dry mustard in a bowl. Gradually add olive oil whisking all the while. Add shallots.

Georgia Gogonelis
La Baguette
567 Erin Drive
Memphis, TN

POMMES DE TERRE A L'HUILE
(French Potato Salad)

8 medium potatoes
3 tablespoons white wine
2 tablespoons chicken stock

½ cup vinaigrette sauce
3 tablespoons shallots, minced
3 tablespoons parsley, minced

Peel and boil potatoes until tender. Slice potatoes into a mixing bowl. Add wine and stock, tossing gently. Add vinaigrette, shallots and parsley. Toss gently.

Georgia Gogonelis
La Baguette
567 Erin Drive
Memphis, TN

19

SALADE NICOISE
(French Chef's Salad)

3 cups green beans, cooked
3 tomatoes, peeled and
    quartered
1 cup vinaigrette sauce
1 head lettuce, washed and
    dried

3 cups French potato salad
3 hard boiled eggs, halved
12 anchovy filets
1 cup canned tuna fish
¼ cup capers
½ cup pitted black olives

Season green beans and tomatoes with vinaigrette. Toss lettuce with vinaigrette. Place lettuce on a large serving platter. Place potato salad in the center. Arrange two mounds of green beans on platter. Surround potato salad with tomatoes. Arrange hard boiled eggs around the platter. Place anchovy filets and capers over eggs. Arrange black olives. Sprinkle all with vinaigrette sauce.

Georgia Gogonelis
La Baguette
567 Erin Drive
Memphis, TN

CHERRIES JUBILEE

1 pound fresh cherries, pitted
    or
1 pound can pitted cherries
1 tablespoon cornstarch mixed
    with

1 tablespoon water, cold
¼ cup Kirsch liquor
¼ cup maraschino liquor
1 quart vanilla ice cream

Drain the cherries and reserve fluid. If using fresh cherries mix ¾ cup water and ¼ cup sugar. Bring this sugar water or the reserved liquid to a simmer. Mash two or three cherries into liquid to color. Gradually, add the cornstarch and water. Cook until thick and smooth. Cool. Heat cherries in a flambé pan, add kirsch and maraschino liquor. Flame, add sauce, and pour cherries and sauce over ice cream.

Georgia Gogonelis
La Baguette
567 Erin Drive
Memphis, TN

COURT BOUILLON

1 cup white wine
2 cups water
1 onion, chopped coarsely
1 carrot, peeled and chopped
   coarsely
2 stalks celery, chopped
   coarsely

1 bay leaf
1 tablespoon fennel seeds
2-3 pepper corns
½ teaspoon salt

Combine all ingredients and simmer 25 minutes. Remove vegetables and discard, saving liquid to prepare the shrimp in CREVETTE AUX CAPRI.

Glen Hays
La Tourelle
2146 Monroe Avenue
Memphis, TN

CREVETTE AUX CAPRI
(Shrimp Marinated with Capers and Onions)

Court Bouillon, 1 recipe
1 pound shrimp, peeled
1 medium onion, sliced thinly
2 ounces capers

1 cup olive oil
3 tablespoons red wine vinegar
1 teaspoon salt
1 teaspoon pepper

Bring Court Bouillon to a boil. drop in the shrimp. Simmer 6-10 minutes until shrimp are pink and firm. Remove shrimp placing them in a bowl with onions and capers. Combine remaining ingredients and pour over the shrimp, onions and capers. Toss lightly. Marinate overnight.

Glen Hays
La Tourelle
2146 Monroe Avenue
Memphis, TN

La Tourelle
French Provincial Cuisine

FRESH STRAWBERRY CREPES

6 cups fresh strawberries,
  sliced (reserve 6 whole
  berries for garnish)
¾ cup brown sugar
6 cooked crepes

2 cups whipping cream,
  whipped
Powdered sugar
½ cup brown sugar

For best results, slice the berries no more than an hour or two ahead of serving time. It is important not to bruise the berries or allow them to go mushy. Toss the sliced strawberries very gently with ¾ cup brown sugar. At serving time, place 1 cup of sliced, sweetened berries in center of each crepe. Top each serving with 2 tablespoons of whipped cream. Sprinkle 1 tablespoon brown sugar (per serving) over whipped cream. Fold sides of crepe over center to enclose whipped cream. Sprinkle 1 teaspoon brown sugar over whipped cream on each serving and top with a whole strawberry. Six servings.

Lee Henderson
The Magic Pan
7720-7722 Poplar Avenue
Germantown, TN

BASIC CREPE

1 cup all-purpose flour
pinch of salt
1½ cups milk

3 eggs
½ cup oil or butter, melted

Stir flour and salt together. Add milk and mix thoroughly forming a thick paste. Add eggs gradually and beat until smooth, the consistancy of heavy cream. Let stand for a half hour. Brush hot pan with butter or oil. Pour in 1½ to 2 tablespoons of the batter, depending upon the pan's size. Tip pan to coat it with a thin layer of batter. When the crepe is golden brown (about one minute) turn and brown the other side. Continue cooking crepes, adding oil or butter as needed. Makes 12 to 14 crepes, 6 to 6½ inches in diameter.

Lee Henderson
The Magic Pan
7720-7722 Poplar Avenue
Germantown, TN

HAM AND ASPARAGUS CREPES

1 (10 ounce) package frozen asparagus (fresh asparagus may be used)	4 thin slices cooked ham
	1 cup Cheddar cheese sauce
	4 cooked crepes
1 tablespoon fresh lemon juice	

Cook asparagus according to package directions. Drain and squeeze lemon juice over spears. Place ham slice in center of crepe. Lay 5 asparagus spears across ham. Fold crepe over filling and place in buttered baking dish (asparagus tips should "peek" out of the ends of the crepe). Heat 10 minutes in 375 degree oven until hot. Top with hot Cheddar cheese sauce or your favorite Hollandaise sauce.

Cheddar Cheese Sauce:

3 tablespoons butter	¼ teaspoon salt
3 tablespoons flour	Dash white pepper
1 cup milk	1 cup grated Cheddar cheese

Melt butter. Stir in flour until smooth. Gradually add milk. Heat to boiling, continuously stirring until sauce thickens. Add remaining ingredients, and stir until cheese melts.

Lee Henderson
The Magic Pan
7720-7722 Poplar Avenue
Germantown, TN

MAGIC PAN SWEET AND SOUR DRESSING (SALAD)

1 teaspoon dried tarragon	½ teaspoon prepared mustard
½ teaspoon salt	½ cup tarragon wine vinegar
⅛ teaspoon pepper	1 cup salad oil
1 tablespoon sugar	

In a small bowl, mix together tarragon, salt, pepper, sugar, and prepared mustard. Using a wire whisk or a fork, beat vinegar with spices to blend thoroughly. Add oil gradually, continuing to beat until mixture is completely blended and dressing has a light, creamy color. Place in refrigerator to allow flavors to blend, about 20 minutes. Makes 1½ cups salad dressing.

Lee Henderson
The Magic Pan
7720-7722 Poplar Avenue
Germantown, TN

POPOVERS

1 cup flour, sifted
¾ teaspoon salt
1 cup milk, cool

1 tablespoon oil or clarified
  butter
2-3 eggs at room temperature

Mix flour and salt together. Add milk and oil together. Add to flour mixture, stir til well combined. Add eggs, one at a time, and mix well after each addition. Beat mixture for 2 minutes more. Warm popover pans and season with vegetable shortening. Preheat oven to 415 degrees. Portion batter ¾ full into each cup. Bake for 30-40 minutes til deep golden brown and sides are very crisp. Remove from oven, slit with knife to let steam out and to crisp popovers inside. Dust with powdered sugar. Serve HOT with butter and jam. Serves 7-8.

Paulette's
2110 Madison Avenue
Memphis, TN

ROBILIO'S ITALIAN SPINACH

2 (10 ounce) packages frozen
  chopped spinach
1 clove garlic, finely minced
¼ cup onion, finely chopped
2 tablespoons parsley, snipped

2-3 tablespoons olive oil
1 tablespoon butter
Salt and pepper to taste
2-3 eggs, beaten
½ cup Parmesan cheese, grated

Cook and drain spinach. Brown garlic, onion and parsley in olive oil and butter. Add spinach, salt and pepper and mix well. Add eggs and Parmesan cheese and stir. Let cook over low heat until firm and brown. Flip and brown other side. Cut into squares to serve.

Marsha Robilio Keller
John P. Robilio
Robilio's Cafeteria
910 Vance
Memphis, TN

VEAL PICCATTA
**this recipe has won the Cuisine Award,
the Epicurean Award and the Travel Holiday Award**

**2 pounds veal, sliced thin and
cut into 2 inch squares
½ cup flour
½ cup butter
juice of 2 lemons**

**1 cup white wine
salt and white pepper
linguine (pasta obtained in a
specialty shop)**

Sprinkle flour over veal: sauté in butter. Slowly add lemon juice and wine (must have balance between butter and lemon juice!) Add salt and white pepper, to taste. Turn once or twice while cooking. Put veal on a hot platter with linguine to side of plate. Cover with Garlic Butter Cream Sauce.

Garlic Butter Cream Sauce:
**¼ pound butter
1 clove garlic, chopped fine
1 tablespoon parsley, chopped
1 cup flour
1 teaspoon monosodium
glutamate**

**juice of one lemon
1 cup white wine
1 quart milk**

Melt butter: sauté garlic 'til light brown. Stir in parsley, flour and MSG. Add lemon juice and wine. Stir in the milk *slowly* or sauce will curdle.

Pete Sciara
Sciara's Palazzino Restaurant
6155 Poplar Avenue
Memphis, TN

BROCCOLI AND CHEDDAR QUICHE

1 9-inch deep dish pie shell
¼ cup onions, diced ¼ inch,
  sautéed and drained
1 cup freshly steamed broccoli,
  diced ¼ inch

4 ounces Cheddar cheese,
  grated
quiche batter (recipe to follow)

Preheat oven to 325 degrees. Pre-bake pie shell in oven for 8 minutes. Place the onions, broccoli and cheese evenly in the pie shell. Fill ¾ full with quiche batter: then, gently spread the ingredients evenly throughout the pie. Place the pie on a sheet pan, then fill to the brim with quiche batter. The pie shell should be completely full. Bake at 325 degrees for 35 to 40 minutes. The pie is done when an inserted knife comes out clean or the pie is firm to the touch in the center. Garnish with fresh parsley and serve with a glass of white wine.

Quiche Batter:
4 extra large eggs
1 cup half and half
½ cup evaporated milk

½ teaspoon salt
¼ teaspoon ground *white*
  pepper

In a suitable sized container, crack the eggs, then add the remaining ingredients and whip with a wire whisk until thoroughly incorporated. Pass the batter through a fine mesh china cap strainer (cone shaped) to remove shell fragments and lumps.

Stan Klaus
Steak and Ale
6201 Poplar Avenue
Memphis, TN

CRABMEAT ST. MORITZ

2 cups fresh mushrooms, sliced
¼ pound sweet butter
2 cups heavy cream
1 cup sherry
4 ounces Beurre Manie (2 ounces butter, 2 ounces flour, kneaded together)
1 pound fresh lump crab meat, picked over
1 cup green onions, diced
salt to taste
white pepper to taste
Worcestershire sauce to taste
Tabasco to taste
lemon juice to taste
6 egg yolks
4 toast rounds
½ cup bread crumbs
½ cup Parmesan cheese, grated

Sauté mushrooms in hot melted butter 'til lightly browned. Add 1½ cups of heavy cream, and 1 cup of sherry. Thicken with Beurre Manie to consistency of heavy cream sauce. Add crab meat and green onions. Season to taste. Make liaison with egg yolks and remaining cream. Add to bubbling sauce and remove from heat. Mix well. Spoon on toast rounds and sprinkle generously with bread crumbs and Parmesan. Bake in preheated oven at 400 degrees for 10 minutes or until brown. Serves 4

Chef Hartmut Kuntze
Otto Gross
Swiss Manor
Germantown, TN

SWISS Manor

SOLE ESCABECHE

6 Filets of Sole (8 ounces each) **salt to taste**
1 lemon **pepper to taste**

Sauce:
½ cup olive oil **2 tablespoons tomato paste**
1 large purple onion, diced **1 teaspoon basil**
coarsely **½ teaspoon thyme**
1 red and 1 green bell pepper, **salt to taste**
cut in julienne strips **pepper to taste**
1 cup fresh mushrooms, sliced **1 tablespoon arrowroot or**
2 tomatoes, peeled and diced **cornstarch**
3 cloves garlic, mashed **1 cup dry white wine**

Heat olive oil in skillet. Sauté each vegetable for 4 to 5 minutes, adding in the following order: onions, bell pepper, mushrooms and tomato. Add garlic, tomato paste and spices. Dissolve arrowroot or cornstarch in white wine and add to sauce. Continue stirring till sauce comes back to a boil. Simmer for a few minutes. Arrange sole in baking dish. Season and broil for 3 to 4 minutes. Pour the sauce over it and finish in preheated oven at 375 degrees for approximately 15 minutes or until fish is done. Sprinkle with chopped parsley and serve with dry rice. Serves 6.

Chef Hartmut Kuntze
Otto Gross
Swiss Manor
Germantown, TN

SWISS Manor

II. Good Eating, Appetizers

Shirley F. Burd and
Linda S. White, Editors

CHEESE BALL

1 pound sharp Cheddar cheese,
shredded
1 (8 ounce) package cream
cheese
½ cup butter or margarine
½ teaspoon HOT Hungarian
type paprika
½ teaspoon onion powder or
garlic powder

1 teaspoon Worcestershire
sauce
parsley, chopped
almonds, chopped
hot paprika
(Variations: minced stuffed
olives (green), or minced
black olives)

Shred cheese using the large hole side of the hand grater. Cut up cream cheese and butter into small pieces and let come to room temperature. Sprinkle with paprika, onion or garlic powder and Worcestershire sauce. Mix well with clean "ringless" hands. Refrigerate until it can be rolled into 3-4 balls. Roll each ball in your choice of covering, parsley, almonds or hot paprika.

·Shirley F. Burd

EDAM CHEESE BALL

1¾ pounds Edam or Gouda
cheese
1 cup beer

¼ cup butter
1 teaspoon celery salt
1 teaspoon dry mustard

Scoop cheese from shell and refrigerate shell. Mix cheese with remaining ingredients until well blended. Put mixture back into shell. Garnish with parsley.

Joyce Djerf

GINGER CHEESE BALL

1 (2 ounce) jar candied ginger
(crystallized)
1 (8 ounce) package cream
cheese, softened

parsley, chopped

Mince the ginger and work into the cheese. Refrigerate in the bowl until cool enough to form into a ball. Roll the ball in the chopped parsley. Wrap the cheese ball tightly in a plastic wrap, excluding all air. Refrigerate until ready to use. Enjoy!

Shirley F. Burd

PARTY CHEESE BALL

3-5 ounces Roquefort cheese
1 (8 ounce) package cream
    cheese
¼ teaspoon garlic salt

1 tablespoon green pepper,
    chopped
1 tablespoon pimiento, chopped
walnuts or pecans, chopped

Blend all ingredients except the nuts and chill until firm. Shape into ball and roll in toasted, chopped walnuts or pecans.

Nell Pewitt

CHEESE WAFERS

1 cup margarine
2 cups flour
pinch salt

½ teaspoon red pepper
8 ounces sharp cheese, grated
2 cups Rice Krispies

Preheat oven to 325 degrees. Cut margarine into the flour with blender or with two knives. Combine flour, salt and pepper. Mix in cheese and fold in Rice Krispies. Pinch off small pieces and place on ungreased cookie sheet and mash flat with a fork. Bake for 15 minutes or until light brown. Makes about 140 wafers.

Dorothy Griscom

ARTICHOKE DIP

1 (14 ounce) can artichoke
    hearts

1 cup mayonnaise
1 cup grated Parmesan cheese

Place all ingredients in blender, including the juice of the artichokes. Puree. Pour into sauce pan. Heat thoroughly. Serve warm with crackers. Melba toast rounds are particularly good with this dip.

Pat Hickman

BROCCOLI DIP

3 boxes of frozen broccoli, chopped
1 medium onion (1½ inches in diameter), minced
½ cup margarine
1 (6 ounce) roll garlic cheese, cut up
2 (10¾ ounce) cans cream of mushroom soup
1 teaspoon monosodium glutamate
salt to taste
1 (4 ounce) can mushrooms, drained

Cook broccoli and drain. Brown minced onion in margarine. Add broccoli, cheese, soup, seasoning and drained mushrooms. Heat until cheese melts. Serve in chafing dish with corn chips.

Margaret Jenkins

CLAM DIP

3-4 ounces cream cheese
1 teaspoon Worcestershire sauce
3-4 dashes hot pepper sauce
½ teaspoon onion powder
1 (6½ ounce) can minced clams, juice drained and reserved.

With cheese at room temperature, mix in sauces and onion powder. Add 2 tablespoons of reserved fluid and mix well. Add the drained clams and mix well. Add additional fluid, a tablespoon at a time, to reach desired consistency. Then, add another tablespoon of fluid as the chilling of the cheese will thicken it slightly. Refrigerate for at least 6 hours to marinate the flavors. Serve with raw vegetables cut to finger food size.

Shirley F. Burd

CLAM DIP II

1 garlic clove
2 (3 ounce) packages of cream cheese
1 teaspoon lemon juice
1 teaspoon Worchestershire sauce
½ teaspoon salt
dash of pepper
½ cup minced canned clams
1 tablespoon clam broth

Rub small mixing bowl with cut halves of a garlic clove. Add cream cheese, lemon juice, Worchestershire sauce, salt, pepper, clams and broth. Blend well. Serve with crackers, chips or raw vegetables to be dipped into the mixture. Makes 1¼ cups.

Margaret Jenkins

CURRY DIP

1 cup mayonnaise
1 teaspoon onion, grated
3 tablespoons catsup
1 teaspoon curry powder

1 garlic clove, cut in half
1 teaspoon Worchestershire
 sauce

Mix together all ingredients. Chill at least 2 hours. Remove garlic and discard. Serve dip with celery sticks, carrot sticks, cauliflower buds and small salad tomatoes.

Armantine Keller

MEXICAN CHEESE DIP

1 (14½ ounce) can tomatoes,
 undrained, cut in small pieces
½ tablespoon garlic powder
½ tablespoon ground cumin
½ teaspoon monosodium
 glutamate

1 or 2 small green onions, cut
 in bits
¼ to ½ teaspoon black pepper
1 jalapeño pepper, seeded
2½ pounds cheese

Put all ingredients, except cheese, in blender and process until well blended. Pour into large sauce pan and bring to boil. Grate cheese and add to sauce, stirring until cheese is melted. Allow to cool. Pour into blender and process until well blended. Add water to each blender full for desired consistency.

Joy Mullins

SHRIMP DIP

1 (8 ounce) package cream
 cheese, softened
1 (10½ ounce) can cream of
 shrimp soup, undiluted

1 (4 ounce) can shrimp bits

Whip cream cheese and soup together. Add shrimp and mix well. Chill. This is great with potato chips.

Peggy Sparrenberger

SHRIMP DIP II

1 clove garlic
¼ cup milk
1 (8 ounce) package cream
  cheese
1 tablespoon lemon juice
⅛ teaspoon Worchestershire
  sauce

1 cup cooked shrimp, finely
  chopped
salt, if desired
parsley, finely minced

Rub small bowl with cut clove of garlic and discard the garlic. Combine milk and cream cheese in bowl and whip together until smooth. Add seasonings and shrimp and blend. Add salt, if desired. Transfer to small serving bowl and sprinkle with parsley. Set on a salad or chip plate or small tray and surround with potato chips, corn chips or crackers.

Dorothy Griscom

SHRIMP DIP III

2 (8 ounce) packages cream
  cheese, softened
½ cup mayonnaise
2 (7½ ounce) cans minced
  clams, juice drained and
  reserved
1 (7½ ounce) can cocktail
  shrimp, drained, juice
  discarded

1 tablespoon Worchestershire
  sauce
onion salt to taste
garlic salt to taste
3 ounces slivered almonds

Cream the cheese and mayonnaise together. Add the drained clams and shrimps. Add 2 to 3 tablespoons of the clam juice, the Worchestershire sauce and seasonings. Blend all together. Serve in a chafing dish. Sprinkle top of dip with slivered almonds.

Lillian Barrett

TANGY PARTY DIP

1 (8 ounce) jar of cocktail sauce
1 (12 ounce) jar of Shedd's or
  Durkee dressing

1 (8 ounce) package cream
  cheese
2 tablespoons horseradish

Mix all ingredients with electric mixer. Serve with raw vegetables.

Mary Pat Van Epps

VEGETABLE DIP

1 teaspoon garlic salt
1 teaspoon curry powder
1 teaspoon tarragon vinegar
1 teaspoon horseradish

1 onion (1½ inch in diameter),
  grated
1 cup mayonnaise

Blend all ingredients. Allow to stand overnight in covered dish in refrigerator. Serve with raw cauliflower, squash, carrots, broccoli, etc.

Dorothy Griscom

EASY SAUSAGE BALLS

3 cups biscuit mix
1 pound hot pork sausage
  (room temperature)

10 ounces sharp Cheddar
  cheese, grated

Preheat oven to 350 - 375 degrees. Crumble the sausage and mix with cheese. Add biscuit mix, one cup at a time. Form into small balls, (about one inch in diameter) and place on an ungreased cookie sheet. (Balls can be frozen now to be cooked later). Bake until light brown (13-15 minutes). Cooking may take a few extra minutes if balls are frozen. Serve warm. Makes about 7 dozen.

Pat Meade

SHRIMP COCKTAIL

2-4 pounds shrimp, peeled and
  deveined
1 (16 ounce) bottle chili sauce

½ cup celery, finely chopped
1 teaspoon horseradish, grated

Cook shrimp in salted water for 3 minutes; cool immediately in ice water. Mix other ingredients in small bowl and refrigerate for several hours. Serve with crackers. Yields 4-6 servings.

Pat Meade

PICKLED SHRIMP

1 pound shrimp
1 cup vinegar
2 tablespoons water
10-12 whole cloves
1 bay leaf

1 onion, sliced
2 teaspoons salt
1 teaspoon sugar
dash of pepper

Mix all ingredients, except shrimp. Boil shrimp in salt water for 5 minutes. (I use those already shelled and deveined.) Drain, cool and add to the above mixture. Let stand in refrigerator 24 hours. Drain and serve with toothpicks.

Note: These keep for a week or two in the refrigerator.

Dorothy Griscom

CRABMEAT APPETIZER

1 (8 ounce) package cream
  cheese, softened
1 tablespoon milk
7 ounces crab meat
2 tablespoons onion, finely
  chopped

1 teaspoon creamed
  horseradish
¼ teaspoon salt
dash pepper
⅓ cup toasted, sliced almonds

Preheat oven to 375 degrees. Mix all ingredients, except the almonds, folding gently to preserve the consistency of the crab meat. Place in an oven-proof dish and sprinkle with almonds. Bake for 15 minutes until bubbly. Serve hot with fancy crackers.

Nancy Willis

CUCUMBER SPREAD

2 medium cucumbers, peeled
1 medium white onion, peeled
1 (8 ounce) package cream
  cheese, softened

½ teaspoon garlic powder
salt and pepper to taste

Shred cucumbers and onion. Drain excess juices. Combine with cream cheese. Add seasonings. Chill. Serve with chips or crackers.

Thelma Williams

SALMON SPREAD

1 (16 ounce) can salmon
1 (8 ounce) package cream
  cheese, softened
1 tablespoon lemon juice
¼ teaspoon salt
1 teaspoon liquid smoke

1 teaspoon Worchestershire
  sauce
½ cup nuts, chopped
3 tablespoons fresh parsley,
  snipped

Drain, bone and flake salmon. Combine with cream cheese, lemon juice, salt, liquid smoke and Worchestershire sauce. Mix well. Shape into a ball on waxed paper. Chill ball. Combine nuts and parsley. Re-shape ball and roll in nuts and parsley. Serve with crackers.

Janet Keller

TUNA-CREAM CHEESE SURPRISE

1 (8 ounce) package cream
  cheese, softened
1 (6½ ounce) can tuna, drained
15-20 stuffed green olives,
  diced

2 tablespoons pickle relish
  (optional)
2 tablespoons dried parsley
  flakes

Mix cream cheese and tuna thoroughly. Cut olives into small pieces. Add to cream cheese and tuna mixture. Add relish and mix thoroughly. Refrigerate about thirty minutes. Form into ball and roll in parsley flakes. Place on cheese board. Serve with crackers. Makes about 25-30 servings.

Barbra Manning

DILLY MARINATED CAULIFLOWER

1 cauliflower
2 tablespoons dill seeds
1 cup sugar
1 cup vinegar

½ cup oil
1 teaspoon salt
1 cup Italian Dressing

Boil cauliflower for five minutes in salted water that includes the dill seeds. Drain cauliflower. Make marinade by combining sugar, vinegar, oil, salt and dressing. Marinate cauliflower for eight hours or overnight.

Lillian Barrett

OLIVE PUFFS

2 cups sharp cheese, grated
½ cup margarine
1¼ cups self-rising flour

1 teaspoon paprika
48 small stuffed olives

Combine cheese, margarine, flour and paprika, chill 15-20 minutes. Mold 1 teaspoon dough around each olive. Chill overnight. Place on baking sheet. Bake at 400 degrees for 10-12 minutes. This is an old family favorite.

Kathryn Morton

SPINACH BALLS

2 (16 ounce) packages frozen
   spinach, chopped
2 cups herb stuffing mix
2 medium onions, grated or
   finely chopped
6 eggs, beaten
¾ cup butter, melted

½ cup dry Parmesan cheese,
   grated
1 tablespoon garlic salt
½ teaspoon thyme
1 tablespoon monosodium
   glutamate
½ teaspoon pepper

Cook spinach according to package directions, drain well. Put into mixing bowl and add all other ingredients. Mix well and refrigerate for 2 hours. Shape mixture into bite size balls. Bake for 20 minutes in 350 degree oven. Yield: Approximately 50 balls. Alternate cooking: Without refrigerating mixture, press into greased baking dish (8"x11"). Bake at 350 degrees for 20 minutes and cut into squares. Serve as hot appetizers.

Sue Dagastino

WHISKEY DOGS

1 pound wieners
¾ cup bourbon
½ cup sugar

½ cup water
½ cup ketchup
1 tablespoon onion flakes

Slice wieners into ½ inch slices. Mix all other ingredients in sauce pan. Stir over low heat until hot. Add wiener slices and continue cooking until thoroughly heated. Serve in chafing dish with toothpicks as hot appetizer.

Sue Dagastino

Beverages

CAFE BAVARIAN MINT

¼ cup powdered non-dairy
   creamer
⅓ cup granulated sugar
¼ cup instant coffee crystals

2 tablespoons powdered baking
   cocoa
2 hard peppermint candies,
   crushed

Put all ingredients in blender container. Cover and process until well blended. Store in airtight container. Use 1 level tablespoon of mix in 6 ounces of boiling water for each cup. Stir well. Yields 14 servings.

Pat Meade

CAFE CAPPUCCINO

⅓ cup powdered non-dairy
   creamer
⅓ cup granulated sugar

¼ cup instant coffee crystals
1 orange-flavored hard candy,
   crushed

Put all ingredients into blender container. Cover and process until well blended. Store in airtight container. Use 1 level tablespoon to 6 ounces boiling water for each cup. Stir well. Serve with large spoonful of whipped cream, if desired. Yields 14 servings.

Pat Meade

CAFE SUISSE MOCHA

¼ cup powdered non-dairy
   creamer
⅓ cup granulated sugar

¼ cup instant coffee crystals
2 tablespoons powdered baking
   cocoa

Put all ingredients into blender container. Cover and process until well blended. Store in airtight container. Use 1 level tablespoon of mix to 6 ounces of boiling water for each one cup serving. Stir well. Serve with large spoonful of whipped cream, if desired. Yields 15 servings.

Pat Meade

CAFE VIENNESE

¼ cup powdered non-dairy
  creamer
⅓ cup granulated sugar

¼ cup instant coffee crystals
½ teaspoon cinnamon

Put all ingredients in blender container. Cover and process until well blended. Store in airtight jar. Use 1 level tablespoon to 6 ounces boiling water for each one cup serving. Stir well. May be served with large spoonful of whipped cream. Yields 14 servings.

Pat Meade

MAMAW'S BOILED CUSTARD

3 quarts milk
14 eggs
2 tablespoons cornstarch

3 cups sugar
lemon extract

In a large heavy pot, heat milk over low heat. In a separate bowl beat eggs. Combine cornstarch and sugar thoroughly and stir into eggs. Add this mixture to milk. Cook, stirring constantly, until the mixture coats a metal spoon. Remove from heat and cool. When cooled, flavor to taste with lemon extract. Store covered in the refrigerator.

Note: This custard will be *thick.* For thinner custard, leave out the cornstarch. Also, you may want to try peppermint flavoring instead of lemon.

Linda White

QUICK EGGNOG OR BOILED CUSTARD

5 cups whole milk
½ cup sugar
1 (3¾ ounce) package instant
  vanilla pudding mix

½ teaspoon vanilla flavor

Mix ingredients thoroughly in mixer or blender. Store in refrigerator. Sprinkle with nutmeg, if desired, before serving.

Note: May add more sugar to taste and more milk to thin. Of course, "nog" may be added for special occasions. Good over strawberries and other fresh fruit.

Joan Dodson

SPICY CRANBERRY PUNCH

¼ cup red cinnamon candies
4 cups water
8 cups (2 quarts) cranberry
  juice cocktail, chilled

1 (6 ounce) can frozen
  lemonade concentrate
1 (6 ounce) can frozen orange
  juice concentrate

Melt cinnamon candies in water in small sauce pan. Chill. At serving time, combine candy liquid and fruit juices in punch bowl. Stir to dissolve frozen concentrates. Float ice chunk in punch bowl. Makes approximately 18 (5 ounce) servings.

Nell Pewitt

CRANBERRY TEA

1 quart water
12 whole cloves
2 cups sugar
1 cup red cinnamon candies

1 quart cranberry juice
juice from 3 lemons
juice from 3 oranges

Mix the water, cloves, sugar, and candies. Cook until the candy melts. Add the cranberry juice and the juice from the lemons and oranges. Refrigerate. When served, dilute with equal amount of water. Serve hot. Makes 16-18 cups.

Margaret Jenkins

RUSSIAN TEA

2 quarts water
½ teaspoon whole cloves
½ teaspoon whole allspice
2 tablespoons loose tea

2 sticks cinnamon
1½ cups sugar
1 cup orange juice
½ cup lemon juice

Boil 2 quarts of water and pour over the cloves, allspice, tea, and cinnamon. Steep 15 minutes, then strain. Add the sugar, orange juice and lemon juice. Serve hot. Makes one-half gallon.

Margaret Jenkins

SPICED TEA

5 quarts water
3 to 5 tea bags (regular - not
   family size)
1 stick cinnamon
1 teaspoon whole allspice
1 teaspoon whole cloves

1 (6 ounce) can frozen orange
   juice concentrate
1 (6 ounce) can frozen
   lemonade concentrate
2 cups sugar

Measure water and pour into large saucepan (I use a large roasting pan). Heat to boiling, then turn off heat. Add tea bags and spices (I put spices in a white baby sock, securing the top with a rubber band or cord). Let steep for 30 minutes. Remove tea bags and spices. Add frozen concentrates and sugar. Stir until all sugar has dissolved. Pour into sterilized glass jugs, cool, and then, refrigerate. Good served hot or cold. Makes 6 quarts.

Note: For a spicy wine cooler, mix with dry white wine or Balloon Wine.

Pat Meade

SPICED TEA MIX

2 cups sugar
2 cups powdered orange-
   flavored breakfast drink mix
1½ cups instant tea

1 (1 quart) package powdered
   lemonade mix
1 teaspoon ground cinnamon
1 teaspoon ground cloves

Put all ingredients in blender container. Cover and process until well blended. Store in airtight container. Use 1 to 2 teaspoons of mix to 6 ounces of boiling water for each cup.

Pat Meade

WASSAIL

½ gallon apple cider
½ gallon cranberry juice
1 stick cinnamon

1 teaspoon whole allspice
½ teaspoon whole cloves

Put cider and juice in large automatic percolator and put spices in percolator basket. Perk juice over spices until percolator turns off automatically. Serves approximately 15-20 people.

Karen Patterson

BAHAMA MAMMA

1¼ ounces rum
3 ounces pineapple juice
¼ ounce orange juice

1 ounce Cream dé Banana
¼ ounce grenadine syrup
dash Triple Sec

Shake well and serve with orange slice and cherry. Yields 1 drink.

Tine Keller

BALLOON WINE

2 (6 ounce) cans frozen grape
  juice concentrate
½ cake yeast or 2 teaspoons
  yeast granules
3 to 4 cups sugar

1 one gallon glass jug, small
  mouth
tap water
1 nine inch balloon

Put grape juice concentrate, yeast and sugar in glass jug. Add tap water to fill jug. Tightly close jug and shake to thoroughly mix contents. Remove cap and replace with balloon. Set jug in a warm, dry place for 6 weeks. The balloon will blow up with gas from fermentation. If balloon pops or blows off, replace. When balloon collapses and jug's contents are clear, wine is ready to be bottled and capped, or poured into a clean jug and stored in refrigerator. When pouring off wine, handle carefully so sediments will not be disturbed. Some sediment in wine will settle out again after bottling. To avoid sediment in bottled wine, siphon into sterilized bottles.

June Ward

BLOODY MARY

1 (46 ounce) can V-8 juice
1 (10 ounce) can of beef broth
1½ soup cans of vodka
salt and pepper to taste

Worchestershire sauce to taste
red pepper sauce to taste
lemon juice to taste

Mix and serve over ice with celery stalk. Makes 10-11, 6 ounce drinks.

Anonymous

HOLIDAY PUNCH

1 quart orange juice
1 quart pineapple juice
1 quart apple juice
15 whole cloves

6 cinnamon sticks
1 cup brown sugar
rum to taste

Mix juices, cloves, cinnamon and brown sugar in a large pot. Heat thoroughly. Cloves and cinnamon sticks may be removed, if desired. Before serving, add rum. (Also tasty without rum.)

Tine Keller

KAHLUA I

1 (½-1 gallon) glass jar
1 (2 ounce) jar Kava coffee
4 cups sugar

1 pint boiling water
1 pint (100-proof) vodka
1 vanilla bean

In jar, mix coffee, sugar and boiling water, dissolving the sugar completely. Add vodka and stir well. Add vanilla bean that has been cut into 1-1½ inch strips. Cover and put aside for one month before serving.

Nancy Herban

KAHLUA II

4 cups water
2 cups sugar
12 level teaspoons instant
   coffee

5 tablespoons vanilla
1 quart cheap vodka

Mix together water, sugar, and coffee and boil for about 1 hour (boils down to about half the original quantity). Cool 3-4 minutes. Add vanilla and vodka. Stir well and bottle. Makes 1¾ quarts.

Note: Tastes better if made 24 hours before serving.

Roberta Mangin

MARGARITA

1 (32 ounce) bottle of lemon
   juice concentrate
1 cup sugar

1 pint hot water
1 ounce tequila
½ ounce Triple Sec

Mix the lemon juice, sugar and hot water. (This can be stored in the refrigerator for later use.) Add one ounce of this mixture to one ounce of tequila and one-half ounce of Triple Sec. Shake with ice and serve in a glass ringed with salt. Makes 10 6-ounce servings.

Anonymous

PHILADELPHIA FISH HOUSE PUNCH

1 quart water
8 teaspoons green tea
1 pint grape juice
1 pint lemon juice
1 pint orange juice
3 lemon peels

¼ pound brown sugar
2 quarts dark rum
1 quart bourbon
1 quart brandy
1 pint peach brandy

Bring water to a boil, add tea, fruit juices, lemon peels, and sugar. Steep 10 minutes. Strain, cool, and add liquors. Let stand, covered, 24 hours before serving. Serve over large chunks of ice in punch bowl.

Anonymous

RUM BAMBOOZLE

2 (20 ounce) cans crushed
   pineapple with juice
2 (46 ounce) cans fruit punch
   drink

1 fifth of rum
2 quarts Sprite

Mix all ingredients and garnish with orange slices, cherries and pineapple chunks. Makes 30 6-ounce drinks.

Tine Keller

SANGRIA

1 bottle red wine
¼ cup brandy

1 (6 ounce) bottle club soda
¼-½ cup sugar

Fill pitcher with ice. Add wine, brandy, club soda, and sugar. Garnish with slices of apple, lemon, and orange. Makes 6-7 6-ounce drinks.

Anonymous

SILVER GIN SLING

1 ounce gin
1 ounce half-and-half
½ ounce lemon juice

1 tablespoon sugar
1 egg white

Blend all ingredients with ice. Use one tray of cubes for 4 servings.

Anonymous

SPIRIT OF THE '80's

1½ ounce bourbon
½ ounce Peter Heering
½ ounce Tia Maria
½ ounce lemon juice

1 ounce pineapple juice
3 ounces orange juice
1 teaspoon lightly beaten egg
   white

Pour all ingredients into tall glass and garnish with lemon slice and cherry. Yields 1 drink.

Tine Keller

WASSAIL BOWL (CIDER PUNCH)

4 cups apple cider
½ cup dark brown sugar,
  packed
½ cup dark rum
¼ cup brandy
1 tablespoon orange liqueur

¼ teaspoon cinnamon
¼ teaspoon ground cloves
⅛ teaspoon allspice
dash of salt
½ lemon, sliced thin
½ orange, sliced thin

Boil cider over moderate heat. Add brown sugar and cook until sugar is dissolved. Remove pan from heat and add rum, brandy, liqueur, spices and fruit slices. Re-heat for 2 minutes and serve hot. Serves 6.

Marion Bendersky

Soups

CHILLED AVOCADO SOUP

3 ripe avocados
1 cup chicken broth
1 cup light cream
1 teaspoon salt

¼ teaspoon onion salt
pinch white pepper
1 teaspoon lemon juice
lemon slices, garnish

Peel avocados and remove seeds. Mash and blend the avocados with chicken broth until smooth. Combine and mix with cream, salt and pepper. Pour into glass container, cover, and refrigerate 3 hours or overnight. Stir in lemon juice, garnish with lemon slices, and serve chilled.

Margaret Jenkins

NAVY BEAN SOUP

1 pound dried Navy beans
1 (3 pound) pork hock
1 medium size onion, chopped
4 carrots, cut up
2 stalks celery, cut up

1 (8 ounce) can tomato sauce
1 teaspoon salt
¼ teaspoon pepper
dash hot pepper sauce

Soak beans overnight, drain. Cover with hot water. Add pork hock and remaining ingredients. Cook over low heat for 5 hours.

Armantine Keller

CLAM CHOWDER I (QUICK)

1 (10¾ ounce) can potato soup
1 (6½ ounce) can chopped
   clams
⅔ cup milk

1-3 dashes hot pepper sauce
2 tablespoons chopped chives
   (fresh, if possible)

Combine soup, clams with their liquid, and milk in a sauce pan. Heat thoroughly and add pepper sauce. Stir thoroughly. Serve with a topping of chopped chives.

Note: This is a great hot item to serve with a cold salad plate during the hot and humid days of the summer.

Shirley F. Burd

CLAM CHOWDER II

3 medium potatoes, diced
1 onion, chopped
2 cups water
2 (6½ ounce) cans minced
   clams, including fluid

2 tablespoons butter
1 pint milk
salt, pepper (cayenne), to taste

Boil potatoes and onion in 2 cups of water for 20 minutes. Add clams and butter. Simmer for 10 minutes. Add milk and seasonings. Reheat and serve.

Shirley F. Burd

SHERRIED CRAB SOUP

2 (10½ ounce) cans cream of
   celery soup
2 (6½ ounce) cans lump white
   crab meat
1 pint half-and-half

milk (amount varies with
   desired consistency of soup)
sherry to taste
salt to taste

Mix cream of celery soup, crab meat, and half-and-half. Add milk to dilute mixture to desired consistency. Add sherry and salt to taste. Cook over low heat 15 to 20 minutes; stir frequently. Do not boil.

Cheryl Stegbauer

EMIKO'S EGG DROP SOUP

1 quart chicken stock
1 tablespoon soy sauce
1 teaspoon salt
½ teaspoon monosodium
   glutamate

2 tablespoons green onions,
   chopped
3 eggs, beaten

To make chicken stock, boil a chicken for 40 minutes to an hour. Skim off residue as it accumulates on top. Remove chicken when tender. To stock add soy sauce, salt, MSG, and green onions. Boil for 3 mintues. Beat the 3 eggs. Pour in a circle into simmering broth. When egg comes to top of the broth, turn off the heat. Serve hot.

Armantine Keller

FRENCH ONION SOUP

3 tablespoons butter
3 large onions, sliced thin
1 tablespoon flour
½ teaspoon salt
freshly ground black pepper
5 cups beef broth

dash of sherry or cognac
4 thick slices French bread
4 tablespoons Parmesan
   cheese, grated
4 tablespoons Swiss cheese,
   grated

In heavy pan, melt butter, add onion and cook slowly until golden. Sprinkle in flour and stir for few minutes to cook. Season with salt and pepper. Add broth, stirring constantly. Bring to a boil, then lower heat and simmer partially covered about 30 minutes. Add dash of sherry or cognac. Toast bread and place in bowls. Preheat broiler. Sprinkle Parmesan cheese on bread. Cover with soup and top with Swiss cheese. Brown under broiler. Serves 4.

Margaret Jenkins

POTATO SOUP

6-8 medium red potatoes
1 large onion, chopped
1 cup water
½ cup (4 ounces) butter

3 cups milk
2 teaspoons salt
1 teaspoon pepper

Boil potatoes in their jackets. (Can be done day before). When cool, peel and dice. Cook onion in water for 15-20 minutes. Add potatoes, butter, salt, and pepper. Add milk to cover potatoes. Heat until steaming but do not boil. Serves 4.

Martha C. Yancey

BLOODY MARY SOUP

1 tablespoon butter
½ cup fresh mushrooms, sliced
½ ounce gin or vodka
1 cup fresh tomato puree
1 cup beef bouillon

squeeze of lemon
1 dash thyme
salt and pepper to taste
1 tablespoon whipping cream

Melt butter and sauté mushrooms. Flambé with gin or vodka. Add puree, bouillon, and lemon and heat through. Add thyme, salt and pepper to taste. Remove from heat and add cream. Serves 2.

Margaret Jenkins

SWISS BEER SOUP

1 cup French bread, cubed,
  crust removed
3 tablespoons oil
1 large onion, chopped
1 clove garlic, minced
1 (12 ounce) can beer (1½ cups)

3 cups chicken broth
½ cup water
2 tablespoons parsley
fresh ground pepper
1 cup Gruyére cheese, grated
1 teaspoon paprika

Toast bread cubes in a 400 degree oven until browned evenly on all sides. Heat oil in large sauce pan over medium heat. Add onion and garlic and cook until onion is limp and gold colored. Stir in bread cubes. Add beer, broth and water and bring to a boil. Add parsley and pepper. Ladle soup into individual heat-proof soup bowls. Divide cheese and sprinkle over soup. Dust with paprika. Heat under broiler until cheese is golden. Serves 4-6.

Pat Hickman

VEGETABLE BEEF SOUP

1 (3 pound) beef roast
4 beef bouillon cubes
1 teaspoon salt
½ teaspoon pepper
3 pounds of canned tomatoes
2 cups celery, cut in chunks
2 large onions, sliced thin
2 tablespoons parsley flakes

1 tablespoon Worchestershire
  sauce
1 teaspoon Lawry's seasoning
  salt
1 teaspoon basil
½ teaspoon thyme
½ pound frozen corn
4 ounces egg noodles

Cook roast in a quart of water with bouillon cubes, salt and pepper until tender. Strain and reserve stock. Remove meat from bone. Add tomatoes, celery, onions, parsley flakes, Worchestershire, Lawry's salt, basil, and thyme to stock. Return meat to soup. Cook on low heat for 1 hour. Add frozen corn and cook 30 minutes more. Add noodles and cook 15 minutes more. Do not boil.

Armantine Keller

HEARTY VEGETABLE BEEF SOUP

1½ pounds stew meat, cut into 1" cubes
3 quarts water, divided
2½ tablespoons salt, divided
½ teaspoon pepper
celery leaves
2 large onions, chopped and divided
2 bay leaves, crushed
¼ teaspoon oregano
¼ teaspoon thyme
1½ cups potato, diced
1 cup carrot, diced
½ pound green beans, cut into 1-2" pieces

4 cups cabbage, shredded
2 (28 ounce) cans tomatoes, undrained
1 teaspoon sugar
1 (17 ounce) can whole kernel corn, undrained
1 (8¾ ounce) can whole kernel corn, undrained
1 (10 ounce) package frozen green peas
1 (10 ounce) package frozen lima beans

Place meat in soup kettle with 2½ quarts water. Add 1 tablespoon salt, pepper, celery leaves and 1 chopped onion. Combine bay leaves, oregano, and thyme; tie in cheesecloth bag and drop into kettle with meat. Cover and simmer for at least three hours. Remove celery leaves. Remove meat from bones, cut into bite size pieces and add to stock. Add potato, carrot, green beans, cabbage, 1 chopped onion and 1 tablespoon salt; simmer for 1 hour. Add 2 cups water, tomatoes, sugar, corn, peas, lima beans and ½ tablespoon salt. Cook an additional hour. Remove cheesecloth spice bag before serving.

Note: This recipe makes about six quarts. Portions may be divided according to need and frozen. Great with cornbread!

Catherine L. Pfeiffer

Salads and
Salad Dressings

AMBROSIA FRUIT SALAD

1 (20 ounce) can pineapple
  chunks
2 (11 ounce) cans mandarin
  oranges
1 (3½ ounce) can flaked
  coconut

1 (5 ounce) package pecan
  halves
2 cups miniature marshmallows
1 (16 ounce) carton sour cream

Drain pineapple and mandarin oranges. Place in large bowl. Add coconut, pecan halves, marshmallows and sour cream. Cover and refrigerate. Serves 8 - 10.

Reba Dye

APRICOT SALAD

1 (3 ounce) package apricot
  gelatin
½ cup pecans, chopped
1 (8 ounce) can crushed
  pineapple, drained
1 cup miniature marshmallows
2 bananas, sliced

½ cup sugar
½ cup pineapple juice
1 egg, slightly beaten
1 (8 ounce) package cream
  cheese
1 package Dream Whip

Mix gelatin per package instructions and add pecans, pineapple, marshmallows and bananas. Allow to jell. Combine sugar, juice, egg and cheese and cook until thickened. Cool and spread over jelled mixture. Prepare Dream Whip according to package directions. Cover with Dream Whip and serve.

Brenda Y. Smith

THREE BEAN SALAD

¾ cup sugar
⅓ cup salad oil
⅔ cup white vinegar
½ teaspoon pepper
½ teaspoon salt, or less
1 (15 ounce) can green beans, drained

1 (15 ounce) can kidney beans, drained
1 (15 ounce) can wax beans, drained
1 medium onion, sliced and rings separated

Combine all ingredients, refrigerate for 24 hours.

Nell Pewitt

GREEN BEAN-TOMATO VINAIGRETTE

1 (8 ounce) can cut green beans, drained
¼ pint cherry tomatoes, cut into halves

1 small onion, sliced
1 (2 ounce) can sliced mushrooms, drained
¼ cup Italian dressing

Toss all ingredients together in a bowl. Cover and chill at least 2 hours, tossing occasionally. Serves two.

Catherine Robertson

BING CHERRY SALAD MOLD

1 (17 ounce) can dark Bing Cherries
1 (15 ounce) can crushed pineapple
1 (3 ounce) package raspberry gelatin
1 (3 ounce) package black cherry gelatin

2 cups Coca Cola
1 cup nuts
1 (8 ounce) package cream cheese, softened and crumbled

Drain juice from cherries and pineapple into a sauce pan and bring to a boil. Remove from heat. Dissolve gelatin in juice. Add the cola and stir. Add the cherries, pineapple and nuts. Crumble in cream cheese and stir well. Pour into molding dish and chill until set.

Armantine Keller

BLUEBERRY SALAD

1 (8 ounce) can crushed
  pineapple
1 (16 ounce) can blueberries
3 (3¾ ounce) packages black
  raspberry gelatin

2 (1½ ounce) packages Dream
  Whip
1 (8 ounce) package cream
  cheese
1 cup nuts, chopped

Drain pineapple and blueberries reserving juices. Add enough hot water to the juices to make 6 cups. Add gelatin and dissolve. Save 2 cups gelatin mixture for the top layer. To the remaining 4 cups, add pineapple and blueberries. Pour into mold and chill until firm. Mix Dream Whip according to package directions. Add cream cheese to Dream Whip and whip until fluffy. Fold in the reserved gelatin, add nuts and pour over firm jello.

Sue Conner

CABBAGE SALAD

3 cups sugar
2 cups vinegar
1 cup water
2 tablespoons salt
2 medium heads cabbage,
  shredded

1 bunch celery, cut fine
2 green peppers, chopped (may
  use 1 red and 1 green)
1 teaspoon celery seed
1 teaspoon mustard seed

Combine sugar, vinegar and water. Boil together 3 minutes and allow to cool. Mix salt into cabbage and let stand (about 15 minutes). Squeeze out excess water. Mix with remaining vegetables and seasonings. Pour cooled liquid over vegetables. Store in refrigerator in closed container. Will keep for 3 weeks. Makes 24 servings (½ cup each).

Margaret Jenkins

CABBAGE SLAW

1 large head cabbage
1 green pepper, chopped
1 large onion, thinly sliced

⅔ cup sugar
⅔ cup salad vinegar
½ cup oil

Chop cabbage coarsely. Add chopped green pepper and onion. Add sugar, vinegar and oil and toss lightly. Marinate in refrigerator for 24 hours, tossing several times.

Kathryn Skinner

CABBAGE OR OTHER RAW VEGETABLE SALAD

1 tablespoon unflavored gelatin
  (1 package)
½ cup cold water
4 tablespoons sugar
½ teaspoon salt

4 tablespoons wine vinegar
1 tablespoon lemon juice
1 cup bouillon (beef or chicken)
1½-1¾ cups shredded cabbage
  (white and red)

Sprinkle gelatin over the cold water in a sauce pan. Heat over low heat, stirring until dissolved. Take from the heat and add the remaining ingredients except for the cabbage. Chill slightly and add the cabbage. Pour into individual molds or one bowl. Chill until firm.

Note: Vary the vegetables, according to the needed color to compliment or contrast with the other food of the meal. The redness of the wine vinegar may be inappropriate for carrots, for example: then, use white vinegar instead of the wine variety.

Shirley F. Burd

GERMAN SLAW

1 medium head cabbage
1 cup sugar
1 cup vinegar
½ cup cooking oil

1 teaspoon salt
1 teaspoon dry mustard
1 teaspoon celery seed

Shred cabbage (may be cut in chunks and put through blender or food processor). If shredded in blender, drain well. Put shredded cabbage in a large bowl, add sugar, stir and set aside. Put vinegar and oil in sauce pan and bring to boil. Add salt, mustard, and celery seed. Pour hot solution over cabbage. Let sit until cool. After slaw has cooled it should be refrigerated in a covered container. This will keep 10 days.

Note: You can also add other ingredients to this recipe such as small onion, grated and one carrot, grated. This can be served same day but is better after 2 or 3 days. If it ends up with too much liquid, simply drain solution after it sits for about 30 minutes. Keep refrigerated after it cools.

Nell Pewitt

HAMBURGER SLAW

½ cup mayonnaise
¼ cup prepared mustard
¼ cup Wesson vegetable oil

1 teaspoon hot pepper sauce
Sugar and salt to taste
Cabbage, finely shredded

Combine and use as dressing on finely shredded cabbage. Good on hamburgers or hot dogs.

Melinda Moore

KRAUT SALAD I

1 quart kraut, drained
½ cup celery, diced
½ cup onion, diced
1 (2 ounce) jar pimiento pieces

½ cup bell pepper, diced
1 cup sugar
1 cup vinegar

Mix all ingredients together and let stand for 2 hours. Yields 6 cups salad.

Melinda Moore

KRAUT SALAD II

1 (1 quart) jar saurkraut
1 cup celery, diced
1 onion, diced
1 green pepper, diced
1 (2 ounce) jar pimiento,
   chopped

1 cup sugar
1 carrot, grated
½ cup vinegar

Mix all ingredients together and let stand in refrigerator overnight.

Mary Pat Van Epps

CHICKEN SALAD

4 cups cooked chicken breasts,
   cut into bite sized cubes
1 cup pecan pieces

1 cup fresh white grapes, whole
½ to 1 teaspoon lemon juice
½ to 1 cup mayonnaise

Mix all ingredients together. Gently spoon salad into lettuce lined bowl or platter. Garnish with extra grapes and whole pecan halves. Serve with homemade hot rolls. Serves 6 to 8.

Catherine Coats

DREAM CHICKEN SALAD

2 cups chicken stock
2 tablespoons unflavored
  gelatin
1 (15½ ounce) can English
  peas, with fluid
4 eggs, hard boiled and
  chopped

2 cups celery, chopped
1 (2 ounce) jar pimiento
1 hen, well cooked, deboned
  and cut into small pieces
1 cup mayonnaise

Heat chicken stock. Dissolve gelatin in cold water. Add to stock. Cool and add other ingredients. Mix well. Add mayonnaise when mixture is cool. Pour into greased 8 x 11 dish and refrigerate until congealed. Cut into squares and serve on lettuce.

Betty Jo Walker

MY CHICKEN SALAD

2 fresh pineapples, cut in half
  and meat scooped out
4 cups white meat chicken,
  cooked and cut into small
  chunks
¾ cup mayonnaise
¼ cup sour cream
⅛ cup coffee cream (half and
  half)
1 small onion (1 inch diameter),
  grated

1 cup celery, chopped
2 eggs, hard boiled and
  chopped
½ cup white seedless grapes
½ cup fresh pineapple (scooped
  from shells), chopped
1 teaspoon curry powder
2 tablespoons soy sauce
¾ teaspoon salt
¼ teaspoon pepper

Combine all above ingredients and mix well. Place in scooped-out pineapple shells and top with mixture below.

Topping for My Chicken Salad:
1 tablespoon butter
3 ounces sliced almonds
½ cup sour cream

4 tablespoons coffee cream
⅛ teaspoon curry powder

Melt butter in small skillet, add sliced almonds and sauté until lightly browned, sprinkle lightly with salt and set aside. Mix sour cream and coffee cream and spoon over salad in pineapple shells, sprinkle with curry powder, then the almonds.

Nancy Willis

CHRISTMAS JELLO

1 (3 ounce) box lime gelatin
1 cup boiling water
1 (15 ounce) can crushed
  pineapple, drained
1 (3 ounce) package cream
  cheese, softened

12 maraschino cherries,
  quartered
½ cup mayonnaise
½ cup nuts
1 (15 ounce) can sweetened
  condensed milk

Dissolve the gelatin in 1 cup hot water. Add remaining ingredients. Mix well. Chill until mixture begins to gel. Remove from refrigerator. Beat mixture. Pour into mold and chill. After removing from mold, garnish with cherry halves. Makes 5 cups.

Joyce Montgomery

COKE SALAD

1 (3¾ ounce) package lime
  gelatin
1 cup hot water
1 (3 ounce) package cream
  cheese

1 cup Coca Cola
½ cup pecans
½ cup crushed pineapple,
  drained

Dissolve gelatin in hot water. Blend in cream cheese. When well blended add Coke. Chill until it starts to thicken, then add nuts and pineapple. Pour into mold.

Pat Meade

CRANBERRY GELATIN SALAD

2 (3 ounce) packages cherry
  gelatin
2 cups boiling water
1 envelope plain gelatin
¼ cup cold water
1 (15 ounce) can cranberry
  sauce

1½ cups cold water
1 (15 ounce) can crushed
  pineapple with juice
¾ cup celery, chopped
½ cup nuts, chopped
1 apple, chopped fine

Dissolve flavored gelatin in boiling water. Soften plain gelatin in ¼ cup cold water and mix this with the flavored gelatin. Add cranberry sauce and 1½ cups cold water and chill until thickened. Add crushed pineapple, celery, nuts, and apple and mix. Chill until set. Good salad with chicken or turkey dishes.

Mary Pat Van Epps

FRUIT SALAD I

2 apples
3 oranges
1 banana
1 pound grapes

3 tablespoons mayonnaise
1 tablespoon sugar
½ cup nuts (optional)

Core and chop apples. Peel and chop oranges. Chop banana. Halve grapes and remove seeds. Mix all ingredients and chill.

Joyce Montgomery

FROZEN FRUIT SALAD II

1 (8 ounce) can crushed
  pineapple
¼ cup maraschino cherries
⅔ cup sugar

2 bananas, mashed
1 cup sour cream
½ cup nuts, chopped

Mix all ingredients and turn into an ice-cube tray and place in the freezer. When frozen, cut into sections and serve on crisp lettuce leaves.

Marie Buckley

FROZEN FRUIT SALAD III

1 (3 ounce) package cream
  cheese, room temperature
½ cup salad dressing
  (mayonnaise)
1 (8 ounce) can crushed
  pineapple

½ cup maraschino cherries,
  chopped
½ green pepper, chopped
½ cup pecans, chopped
1 cup whipping cream, whipped

Mash cream cheese and blend with mayonnaise. Add pineapple, cherries (cut in pieces), chopped green pepper, and chopped nuts. Fold in the whipped cream and turn into ice cube tray and place in the freezer. When frozen serve on crisp lettuce leaves.

Note: This should freeze in about 2 hours; if left too long, it will become icy.

Marie Buckley

LOW CALORIE MARINATED FRUIT

1 (20 ounce) can pineapple
  chunks
1 medium red apple
1 medium green apple
1 medium pear

1 banana, sliced
2 tablespoons orange juice
1 tablespoon honey
1 teaspoon mint, crushed or 1
  teaspoon mint extract

Drain pineapple; reserve juice. Remove cores from apples and pear. Slice into chunks. Slice banana. Mix fruit in shallow dish. Mix reserved juice with orange juice, honey and mint. Pour over fruit. Cover, marinate in refrigerator 2 to 3 hours. Stir occasionally. Serve in clear dishes with marinade. Serve 8.

Martha C. Yancey

LIME CHEESE SALAD

**1 (6 ounce) package lime
gelatin**
1 (16 ounce) carton Cool Whip
**1 (20 ounce) can crushed
pineapple, drained**

**1 (8 ounce) carton small curd
cottage cheese**

Prepare gelatin per package directions (juice from crushed pineapple may be used for part of cold water). Let gelatin chill until thick but not set. Fold in other ingredients. Pour into 8 x 11 inch dish, refrigerate until firm. Halved red or green cherries may be used for decoration.

Dianna Thompson

MACARONI SALAD I

**1 pound small salad style
macaroni**
**¾ pound processed cheese, cut
up**
**1 large or 2 small fresh
cucumbers, chopped**
1-1½ green peppers, chopped
**1-2 cups mayonnaise, enough
to mix**

6 hard boiled eggs, chopped
**1 (4 ounce) jar mushroom
pieces**
**⅓-½ cup sweet pickle relish,
drained**
½ teaspoon salt, or to taste
⅛ teaspoon pepper, or to taste

Cook macaroni as directed on package, drain. While still hot, stir cheese into macaroni and allow to melt. Add all other ingredients, mix well and chill.

Note: Makes a lot, small amounts are never enough for your guests.

Dianne Thompson

MACARONI SALAD II

1 (8 ounce) package elbow
  macaroni
1 cup celery, diced
½ cup green pepper, diced
½ cup French salad dressing
½ cup mayonnaise

½ cup sour cream
1 teaspoon prepared mustard
½ teaspoon salt
¼ cup parsley, chopped
Romaine lettuce to line bowl

Cook macaroni as directed on package. Drain. Add celery and green pepper. Pour French dressing over macaroni. Chill several hours or overnight. Before serving, mix mayonnaise, sour cream, mustard and salt. Fold gently into macaroni. Add parsley. Spoon into serving bowl lined with Romaine lettuce.

Jo Pool

MOLDED GARDEN SALAD

1 (3 ounce) package lemon
  gelatin
2 tablespoons lemon juice or
  white vinegar
¼ cup green onions, chopped

½ cup cucumbers, diced
½ cup radishes, sliced thin
½ cup celery, chopped
½ cup raw cauliflowerets

Prepare gelatin according to package directions, add vinegar or lemon juice. Pour in 6 cup mold, chill. When partially set, add vegetables. Serve when fully set. Serves 6.

Patricia D. Hallmark

NASHVILLE SALAD

1 (8 ounce) package cream
  cheese, softened
1 (16 ounce) can crushed
  pineapple

1 (16 ounce) carton Cool Whip
1 (16 ounce) bag colored
  marshmallows
½ cup nuts, chopped

Cream together cream cheese and juice from pineapple. Fold in Cool Whip and marshmallows, add chunk pineapple. Add nuts. Also is pretty with 4 ounces of red or green cherries, sliced. Refrigerate. Yields 8 to 10 servings.

Pat Meade

SOUR CREAM POTATO SALAD

6 large potatoes, boiled in
   jackets, cooled and peeled
Salt and pepper
4 eggs, hard boiled and
   chopped

1 large onion, chopped
1 (10 ounce) jar sweet relish
1 (8 ounce) carton sour cream
paprika

Cube potatoes into mixing bowl. Add salt and pepper to taste. Add chopped eggs and onion. Mix in relish and sour cream to coat potatoes. Place in serving bowl and sprinkle with paprika.

Margaret Jenkins

CONFETTI RICE SALAD

1 cup rice (not precooked)
8 cups boiling water
1 cup crushed pineapple,
   drained
½ pint half and half

½ (5-6 ounce) package salad
   marshmallows
½ cup maraschino cherries,
   chopped
½ cup walnuts, chopped

Add rice to boiling water. Cook until done. Drain and cool. Add other ingredients. Mix and set overnight in refrigerator.

Joyce Montgomery

SALAD WITH SWEET AND SOUR DRESSING

3 tablespoons vinegar
6 tablespoons oil
2 tablespoons honey
1 teaspoon Dijon style mustard
½ teaspoon salt
dash of pepper

1½ teaspoons poppy seeds
1 pound fresh spinach or red-
   tipped lettuce
4 green onions, chopped finely
1 (11 ounce) can mandarin
   oranges, drained

Thoroughly mix vinegar, oil, honey, mustard, salt, pepper and poppy seeds. Toss spinach and chopped onions with above mixture. Top with drained mandarin oranges.

Note: A wire whisk works well for mixing dressing.

Cheryl Stegbauer

7-UP SALAD

1 (10 ounce) package
marshmallows
8 ounces 7-Up
1 (3 ounce) package lime
gelatin
1 (8 ounce) package cream
cheese

1 (15 ounce) can crushed
pineapple
1 cup nuts, chopped
1 (8 ounce) carton Cool Whip

Over low heat dissolve marshmallows with 7-Up. Add gelatin and stir until dissolved. Add cream cheese. Blend in electric blender for several seconds. Remove and fold in pineapple with juice and nuts. Pour in mold and place in refrigerator for 40 minutes. Remove and fold in Cool Whip. Chill 1 hour.

Anne Nelson

ORANGE SHERBET SALAD

1 (6 ounce) package orange
gelatin
1½ cups water, boiling
2 cups orange sherbet
1 (15 ounce) can crushed
pineapple, drained

1 (11 ounce) can mandarin
oranges, drained
2 bananas, sliced

Dissolve gelatin in boiling water and juice from drained fruit that equals 2 cups. Stir in sherbet and let set for a few minutes. Add pineapple, oranges, and bananas. Pour into mold or rectangular dish and place in refrigerator until set. May be served as a salad with cheese crackers or as a dessert with whipped topping.

Note: Different gelatin flavors can be used.

The Committee

SIX CUP SALAD

1 (11 ounce) can Mandarin
oranges
1 (8 ounce) can crushed
pineapple

1 cup sour cream
1 cup small marshmallows
1 cup coconut
1 cup nuts, chopped

Combine all ingredients; mix well and allow to stand covered overnight.

Margaret Jenkins

SHRIMP SALAD

2½ cups elbow macaroni
1½ pounds cooked shrimp
  (small or cut up)
⅔ cup celery, chopped
1 medium onion, chopped
1 cup mayonnaise

½ cup sweet pepper relish
2 tablespoons lemon juice
2-3 dashes hot pepper sauce
½-¾ teaspoon salt
¼-½ teaspoon pepper

Cook macaroni according to package directions, drain and cool. Mix together macaroni, shrimp, celery and onion. Mix together the remaining ingredients. Combine the two mixtures and stir well. Chill, preferably for 24 hours to marinate the flavors. Serve in a lettuce lined bowl. Serves 8-10.

Shirley F. Burd

CONGEALED VEGETABLE SALAD

¾ cup sugar
½ teaspoon salt
½ cup vinegar
1 cup water
2 envelopes plain gelatin
½ cup cold water
1 cup celery, chopped
½ cup black olives, sliced
2 cups asparagus pieces (or cut
  green beans), cooked and
  cooled

1 (2 ounce) jar pimiento, diced
½ medium onion, chopped
juice of ½ lemon
½ cup sour cream
½ cup mayonnaise
½ teaspoon paprika
onion juice to taste

Combine sugar, salt, vinegar, and water and boil for 5 minutes. Dissolve gelatin in cold water and add to hot vinegar solution. Chill until mixture starts to become firm. Meanwhile, combine celery, olives, asparagus, pimiento, onion, and lemon juice. Fold into gelatin mixture and place in refrigerator in a 9 or 10 inch square dish. Cover with plastic wrap. When salad is congealed and ready to serve, make a topping of sour cream, mayonnaise, paprika and onion juice (you may want to vary the proportions). Spread topping over salad and cut into squares for serving on lettuce.

Linda White

MARINATED VEGETABLE SALAD

1 (14 ounce) can cut asparagus
   spears, drained
1 (15 ounce) can cut green
   beans, drained
½ pound fresh mushrooms,
   sliced
1 pint cherry tomatoes,
   quartered
¼ cup red wine vinegar
¼ cup vinegar
½ cup oil
1 tablespoon Dijon style
   prepared mustard

⅛ teaspoon dried tarragon
6-8 green onions, chopped
¼ cup fresh parsley, minced
1 clove garlic, minced fine (or ¼
   teaspoon garlic powder)
2 stalks celery, chopped
1 tablespoon fresh lemon juice
1 teaspoon salt
¼ teaspoon pepper
3 dashes cayenne pepper
¼ cup sugar
1 egg, hard boiled and chopped

Place asparagus, green beans, mushrooms and tomatoes in a large bowl. Combine all other ingredients, except the egg, in a jar and shake well. Pour over vegetables and marinate overnight. Before serving, sprinkle with chopped egg.

Tine Keller

WATERGATE SALAD

1 (3¾ ounce) package pistachio
   instant pudding mix
1 (15 ounce) can crushed
   pineapple

1 cup miniature marshmallows
1 (8 ounce) carton Cool Whip

Mix pudding with pineapple and juice. Blend in remaining ingredients. Pour into a 13 x 9 dish and spread evenly. Chill overnight. Cut into squares and serve on lettuce leaves.

Melinda Moore

FRENCH DRESSING

1 (10¾ ounce) can tomato soup,
   undiluted
½ cup sugar
½ cup vinegar

½ cup oil
1 tablespoon onion, grated
1 teaspoon paprika

Mix all ingredients. Bring to a boil over medium heat. Let cool before using.

Pat Worley

FRENCH DRESSING FOR SPINACH SALAD

1 cup salad oil
¾ cup sugar
¼ cup vinegar
⅓ cup ketchup
1 clove garlic
1 tablespoon Worchestershire
  sauce

squirt of fresh lemon
½ onion, quartered
fresh spinach
fresh mushrooms, sliced
bacon, cooked and crumbled
egg, hard boiled and diced

Place oil, sugar, vinegar, ketchup, garlic, Worchestershire sauce, lemon juice and onion in blender and blend until onion is cut up fine. Serve over spinach, mushrooms, bacon and egg salad.

Armantine Keller

MAMA'S GARLIC DRESSING

1 cup granulated sugar
1 cup vegetable oil
1 cup cider vinegar
1 tablespoon dry mustard
1 teaspoon black pepper

1 tablespoon salt
1 tablespoon lemon juice
1 (10½ ounce) can tomato soup,
  undiluted
2 cloves garlic, peeled

Combine all ingredients in blender and blend well. Refrigerate and serve over tossed salad. Makes 1 quart.

Patricia D. Hallmark

HONEY LIME DRESSING

8 ounces mayonnaise
2 ounces lime juice
1 ounce powdered sugar

2 ounces honey
6 ounces heavy cream, whipped

Combine mayonnaise, lime juice, and sugar with honey. Fold into whipped cream carefully. Do not over mix. Honey, lime juice and sugar may be adjusted to taste. Serve over fresh fruit.

Pat Worley

MINT VINEGAR

¼ cup dried mint, or ½ to ¾
   cup fresh mint leaves
2 cups white vinegar

½ cup granulated sugar or
   equivalent in sugar substitute
green food coloring

Crush the mint leaves, if using the fresh variety. Heat vinegar with sugar and mint leaves. Simmer uncovered for at least 15 minutes. Strain through a cheesecloth into a sterilized jar or bottle.

Note: Should the shade of green not be to your liking, add food coloring one drop at a time, stirring well after each addition. (This usually is done when using the dried mint leaves). Serve in your most attractive cruet for salads. Use some other vinegar if you want an oil-and-vinegar dressing.

Shirley F. Burd

RICHARD'S SALAD DRESSING

5 or 6 green onions, chopped
¼ cup salad oil
¼ cup garlic vinegar
¼ teaspoon pepper
1 teaspoon dried parsley

1 teaspoon salt
1 teaspoon monosodium
   glutamate
½ teaspoon oregano
½ teaspoon garlic powder

Combine all ingredients and chill.

Tine Keller

HOMEMADE THOUSAND ISLAND DRESSING

1½ cups mayonnaise
¾ cup ketchup
½ onion, chopped fine
1 egg, hard boiled

¾ cup pickle relish
⅛ teaspoon black pepper
⅛ cup celery, chopped
   (optional)

Mix all ingredients by hand. Serve over crisp salad greens mixed with your favorite salad additions.

Tine Keller

Beef and Pork

BEEF STROGANOFF

2 pounds beef tenderloin or
  sirloin steak
¼ cup margarine
3 (2½ ounce) jars sliced
  mushrooms, drained
  (save fluid)
2 (10½ ounce) cans condensed
  broth (beef)

½ cup instant onion flakes
⅓ cup ketchup
2 teaspoons garlic salt
1½ teaspoons flour
  (Wondra preferred)
1 pint sour cream
10 ounces egg noodles
3 tablespoons margarine

Prepare meat cutting across the grain in ¾ inch slices, and then into strips measuring 3 x ¼ inch. Brown meat in iron skillet or dutch oven using ¼ cup margarine. Reserve ½ cup broth. Mix in the remaining broth, fluid from mushrooms, onion, ketchup and garlic salt. Simmer 15-20 minutes. Blend reserved broth with the flour and stir into meat. Add mushrooms and heat to boiling, stirring constantly. Boil and stir for one minute and add sour cream. Heat thoroughly—but do not boil. Cook noodles according to package directions. Drain and toss with margarine until melted. Pour stroganoff over noodles. Serve with a salad, rolls and wine of choice. 6-8 servings.

Note: See Jim Bown's Noodle recipe.

Shirley F. Burd

"BOILED DINNER" OR CORNED BEEF AND VEGETABLES

4½ pounds lean corned beef
8 medium potatoes, scrubbed
8 small turnips, scrubbed
8 small to medium onions,
  peeled

16 medium carrots, scrubbed
1 large cabbage, cut 6-8 wedges
mustard and horseradish,
  to taste

Cover beef with boiling water and boil at a slow boil for 1 hour. Drain and cover again with boiling water. Bring to a boil and simmer for 2½ hours. Add vegetables, except cabbage, simmering until done, (20-30 minutes). Add cabbage to top to allow it to steam for about 20 minutes. In a separate dish, combine mustard and horseradish to taste and serve as sauce. Use cooking liquid as another sauce. Serve with rolls or french bread and an optional salad. Serves 6-8.

Note: This may be cooked in the pressure cooker using the cooker directions and cooking the meat and vegetables separately. The cooker does save time and energy. When cold, thinly slice the leftover corned beef for sandwiches.

Shirley F. Burd

BULKOGI (KOREAN DISH)

3 pounds beef, sliced in ⅛ inch
   thickness
½ cup Soya sauce (Kikoman
   Japanese Sauce)
¼ cup green onion, chopped
¾ cup water
3-4 tablespoons sugar

2 teaspoons sesame oil
½ teaspoon garlic powder or
  1 teaspoon garlic, chopped
½ teaspoon black pepper
¼ teaspoon monosodium
   glutamate

Mix soya sauce and rest of the seasonings. Add sliced beef and marinate for at least 3-4 hours (may marinate overnight). Broil 3-4 minutes on each side. Serve with steamed rice.

Katherine Kim

PRIME RIB OF BEEF

12 pounds prime rib of beef
  (boned and rolled)

salt and pepper to taste

Remove roast from refrigerator at least 30 minutes prior to cooking. Wipe meat with damp cloth, sprinkle with salt and pepper (approximately ¾ teaspoon salt per pound). Brown on 3 sides in an iron skillet; place roast, fat side up, in 350 degree oven, uncovered. Bake 15 minutes per pound. Cut off heat, cover and leave in oven for 30 minutes.

Marie E. Buckley

MATAMBRE
(BEEF WITH CHILI SAUCE)

2 (2 pounds each) flank steaks,
butterfly cut
1 cup frozen mixed vegetables,
thawed
½ cup onion, chopped fine
¼ cup green pepper, chopped
fine
½ cup pimiento, chopped fine
2 teaspoons chili pepper,
chopped fine, or 1-2
teaspoons chili powder

1 clove garlic, crushed
1 teaspoon salt
1 cup beef broth
1 celery stalk
1 carrot, sliced
1 medium onion, sliced
1 clove garlic, chopped

Pound steaks as thin as possible. Lay steaks side by side overlapping 2 inches so they make a long strip. Combine and mix vegetables, onion, green pepper, pimento, chili pepper, chili powder, and garlic. Spread mixture over steak. Roll steak like a jelly roll and tie as tight as possible every 1-2 inches. Put roll in shallow casserole and add salt, beef broth, celery, carrot, onion and garlic clove. Cover and braise in a 350 degree oven for 2 hours, basting several times. Move to platter 15 minutes before serving to make carving easier. Slice and serve with chili sauce. Serves 6.

CHILI SAUCE FOR MATAMBRE

4 tablespoons butter
1 onion, chopped fine
1 green pepper, chopped fine
1 clove garlic, minced
2 tablespoons flour

1 tablespoon chili powder
1 teaspoon salt
fresh ground pepper to taste
1 cup tomato juice
1 cup beef broth

Melt butter in medium skillet. Sauté onion, green pepper and garlic until vegetables are translucent, about 5 minutes. Blend in flour, chili powder, salt and pepper and stir over low heat for 3 minutes. Stir in juice and broth, cook and stir until thickened. Serve hot over Matambre at table.

Pat Hickman

SECRET ROAST RECIPE

3 to 5 pounds boneless rump
 roast

1 package onion soup mix
2 tablespoons water

Wash roast thoroughly in cold water; do not dry. Place on top of double layer of aluminum foil. Sprinkle soup mix over roast and add water. Seal foil around roast so that fluid will not leak out. Bake in 350 degree oven for about 3 hours or until tender. 30 minutes before serving, turn the foiled roast upside down so juices will marinate the roast. Drippings can be thickened for gravy.

Mary Anderson

SWEDISH POT ROAST

3-4 pound chuck roast
cinnamon, to taste
ginger, to taste
nutmeg, to taste
salt to taste
pepper to taste
3 medium onions, sliced in
 eighths

1 garlic clove, minced
½ cup vinegar
½ cup brown sugar
1 cup water
1 bay leaf
3-4 potatoes, scrubbed and
 sliced
3 carrots, sliced

Preheat oven to 400 degrees. Rub roast generously with cinnamon, ginger, nutmeg, salt and pepper. Brown meat on all sides. Add onions and garlic. Mix vinegar and brown sugar and pour over meat. Add water and bay leaf. Cover and bake for 2 hours. Add potatoes and carrots and cook 30 minutes longer. Add more water if needed.

Mary Pat Van Epps

STEAKS A LA MILANESE

2 tablespoons butter, divided
½ teaspoon rosemary
4 filet mignons
¼ teaspoon dry mustard

¼ teaspoon Worcestershire
  sauce
3 tablespoons Cognac

Melt one tablespoon butter with rosemary in heavy skillet or use electric skillet as desired. Do not let butter brown. When rosemary has flavored butter well, add meat and cook to taste, turning meat from time to time. When meat is done, remove to hot platter. Add remaining butter, mustard, Worchestershire sauce and Cognac to pan. Let heat thoroughly, but do not boil. Pour over meat and serve immediately. Serves 4.

Mary L. Shannon

STEAKS WITH CUBAN MARINADE

1 cup red wine vinegar
⅓ cup orange juice
4 drops hot pepper sauce
¼ teaspoon pepper

½ cup onion, finely chopped
4 large cloves garlic, minced
2 tablespoons vegetable oil
steaks of choice

Mix all ingredients. Score steaks and marinate in refrigerator 3-5 hours, turning meat occasionally. Broil steak using marinade as a basting sauce.

Patricia D. Hallmark

TENDERLOIN OF BEEF WELLINGTON

3 pounds beef tenderloin
  (possibly, eye of round)
2 tablespoons soft butter or
  margarine
1 teaspoon salt
½ teaspoon pepper

3 pie crust sticks or pastry for
  3 pie shells
mushroom Filling
1 egg
1 tablespoon water
Brown Sauce

Heat oven to 425 degrees. Tie a heavy string at several places around the meat. Place on a rack in a shallow pan. Spread butter over top and sides of meat and sprinkle with salt and pepper. Bake for 20 minutes. Place on a cooling rack for 30 minutes. Remove string and pat meat dry. Prepare pastry according to package directions. Roll pastry out on foil into a 24x18 inch rectangle. Cut to this size. Use excess pastry to cut out small designs of stars, flowers, crescents, whatever, and reserve. Place the meat at the edge of the 24″ side of the pastry. Spread the mushroom filling over the remainder of the pastry, leaving a 1" margin at the edges. Roll tenderloin and pastry. Seal the seam and ends securely (moistening with water) and place the seam underneath when the roll is placed on a baking sheet. Garnish with the cutouts of pastry. Mix the egg and water and brush top and sides of roll. Preheat oven to 400 degrees and bake 30 minutes until pastry is golden brown. Serve with Brown Sauce. Serves 8. (This can be prepared ahead and the last of the baking done while guests congregate).

Mushroom Filling for Beef Wellington:

1 pound fresh mushrooms, finely chopped
½ cup onion, finely chopped
½ cup dry sherry
¼ cup butter or margarine
¼ cup fresh parsley, finely chopped

Cook together and stir the ingredients until the onion is done and all liquid is absorbed. Use for filling of the Tenderloin of Beef Wellington.

Brown Sauce for Beef Wellington:

2 cups beef bouillon
½ cup dry sherry
3 tablespoons onions, finely chopped
3 tablespoons carrots, finely chopped
1 tablespoon celery, finely chopped
2 sprigs parsley, finely chopped
1 bay leaf, crumpled
⅛ teaspoon thyme
3 tablespoons dry sherry
2 tablespoons butter or margarine

Combine bouillon, ½ cup sherry, vegetables and spices and simmer for 30 minutes. Strain mixture through a fine sieve. Stir in the 3 tablespoons of dry sherry and simmer for 5 minutes. Cut butter into small pieces and stir into sauce. Serves as a sauce for the Tenderloin of Beef Wellington.

Shirley F. Burd

SUKIYAKI

1 pound beef, cut in thin slices
1-2 medium onions, cut in thin slices
4-5 green onions, cut in 2 inch lengths
10 mushrooms, fresh or dried, cut in thin slices
1 cup spinach (may use celery)
1 cup bamboo shoots

1 carrot, cut in 2 inch long thin slices
½ cup soya sauce
2 tablespoons sugar
½ cup water
pepper (optional)
monosodium glutamate
½ cup bean thread

Place all ingredients except bean thread in roasting pan. Mix soya sauce and sugar with ½ cup of water; pour into pan. Season with pepper and accent. Cook at 300 degrees until meat is tender. Soak bean thread (transparent noodle) in warm water and drain. Add bean thread about 15 minutes before serving. Makes 4-5 servings. Serve with steamed rice.

Katherine Kim

WINE MARINADE FOR STEAK

2 pounds sirloin
12 large, fresh mushrooms
½ cup Burgundy
1 teaspoon Worcestershire sauce
1 clove garlic, minced
½ cup salad oil
2 tablespoons ketchup

1 teaspoon sugar
½ teaspoon salt
½ teaspoon monosodium glutamate
1 tablespoon vinegar
½ teaspoon marjoram
½ teaspoon rosemary

Cut steak into pieces to fit on skewer. Clean mushrooms and reserve. Mix wine and other ingredients together. Add the steak pieces and mushrooms to the marinade. Marinate for at least 2 hours, turning several times. If steak and mushrooms are allowed to marinate for 8-12 hours or longer, the flavor is enhanced! Serves 4.

Tine Keller

BEAN AND HAMBURGER BAKE

½ pound ground beef
¼ cup onion, diced
¼ cup green pepper, diced
½ cup ketchup
1 tablespoon mustard

1 tablespoon Worcestershire
  sauce
¼ cup syrup or molasses
1 (14 ounce) can pork and
  beans

Brown meat, onion and green pepper in skillet. Drain off fat. Add all other ingredients and mix well. Turn into casserole and bake at 350 degrees for 30-45 minutes. Serves 4 to 6.

Carolyn Foster

BEEF AND BEAN CASSEROLE

1 pound ground beef
¼ cup green pepper, chopped
½ teaspoon garlic salt
1 (16 ounce) can or 1¾ cups
  baked beans

1 (8 ounce) can tomato sauce
1 (4 ounce) can mushroom
  stems and pieces, drained

Brown ground beef, green pepper and garlic salt. Pour off fat. Stir in beans, tomato sauce and mushrooms; heat until bubbly. Spoon mixture into two quart casserole. Top with mixture below.

Topping:
1 cup pancake mix
¾ cup sour cream

¾ cup cheddar cheese, grated
1 tablespoon sesame seeds

In medium sized bowl (1 quart) combine pancake mix with sour cream and cheese, blend well. Spoon mixture around edge of hot meat mixture. Sprinkle with sesame seeds. Bake in 375 degree oven, uncovered, for 25 to 30 minutes, until topping is golden brown. Serves 6.

Catherine Robertson

MEATY BAKED BEANS

1 pound ground beef
1 cup onion, chopped
1 green pepper, chopped
2 (16 ounce) cans pork and
  beans
6 ounces tomato ketchup

1 teaspoon Worcestershire
  sauce
1 tablespoon mustard
½ cup brown sugar
1 teaspoon salt
½ teaspoon black pepper

Brown the ground beef, onion and green pepper in skillet or sauce pan. Pour off fat. Combine all ingredients in a casserole dish or bean pot. Mix well. Bake in a 350 degree oven, uncovered, for 30 minutes. Cover and cook an additional 30 minutes. Serves 8 to 10. May be used as a main dish or side dish.

Dianne Greenhill

THREE BEAN - BEEFY CASSEROLE

1 pound ground beef
1 small onion (1 inch diameter),
  chopped
1 (15 ounce) can red kidney
  beans, drained
1 (15 ounce) can lima beans,
  drained

1 (15 ounce) can pork and
  beans, not drained
½ cup ketchup
½ cup brown sugar
2 tablespoons vinegar
½ teaspoon salt

Brown beef and onion in skillet and drain off excess fat. Combine with remaining ingredients and turn into 1½ quart casserole. Bake in 350 degree oven for one hour.

Lynne Gorline

DAGO'S DELIGHT

1 (7 ounce) package egg
  noodles
1 sweet pepper, diced
1 medium onion, diced
1 clove garlic, diced
1 pound ground beef
½ teaspoon salt
⅛ teaspoon pepper

1 (17 ounce) can creamed corn
1 (10¾ ounce) can cream of
  mushroom soup
1 (7 ounce) can mushroom
  slices
1 (8 ounce) can tomato sauce
6 slices processed American
  cheese

Boil noodles in water until tender; drain. Brown sweet pepper, onion and garlic in oil. Add ground beef, cook until only lightly brown. Drain off oil. Pour into large bowl and fold in noodles and all other ingredients except cheese. Pour into 9x12 baking dish and top with cheese slices. Bake at 350 degrees until cheese browns, 15-20 minutes. Serve hot. Yields 6-8 servings.

Janna Young

HAMBURGER CASSEROLE

2 pounds ground beef or
  ground chuck
2 or 3 medium sized (2 inches
  in diameter) potatoes
2 to 4 carrots

1 (16 ounce) can English peas,
  drained
1 medium sized (1½ to 2 inches
  in diameter) onion

Season ground beef to taste as for hamburgers. Shape beef into patties and arrange to cover bottom of baking dish. Peel and thinly slice potatoes, arrange slices over beef patties. Scrape and slice carrots, arrange slices over potatoes. Pour drained peas over carrots. Slice onion and arrange over peas. Cover dish with foil and bake in 400 degree oven for 1½ hours. Serves 6 to 8.

Melinda Moore

CHILI—HOT! HOT! HOT!

2 pounds ground chuck
1 teaspoon salt
1 teaspoon pepper
1 clove garlic, chopped
1 teaspoon garlic powder
1 large Bermuda onion,
  chopped
1 large green bell pepper,
  chopped
2 stalks celery, including the
  leaves, chopped

3½ tablespoons chili powder
3 tablespoons Worcestershire
  sauce
2 large banana peppers
2 dashes of red pepper sauce
2 ounces water
1 (12 ounce) can tomato paste
1 (15 ounce) can tomato sauce
2 (15 ounce) cans red kidney
  beans
2 cups water

Brown meat with salt, pepper, chopped garlic and garlic powder, stirring occasionally. Put chopped onion, bell pepper and celery in a bowl. Sprinkle these vegetables with chile powder and Worcestershire Sauce. Mix well. Combine the two mixtures, cooking for 30 to 40 minutes. In a blender, combine the banana peppers, the red pepper sauce and the water. Liquify and add to mixture. Add the tomato paste, tomato sauce, red beans and water. Simmer for 3 hours. Serves six.

Shirley F. Burd

MOM'S CHILI (MILD)

2 tablespoons corn meal
2 tablespoons chili powder
1 tablespoon salt
1 tablespoon sugar
⅛ teaspoon oregano
⅛ teaspoon cumin
1 medium-large onion, chopped

1 pound lean ground beef
1 clove garlic, minced
1 (6 ounce) can tomato paste
1 (15 ounce) can beans in chili
  gravy
42 ounces water

Mix all dry ingredients together and set aside. Cook chopped onion in just enough melted shortening or oil to keep from sticking to the pan. Cook onions only until they begin to look clear. Do not brown! Add ground beef and cook until it loses its red color. Add garlic. (If you do not have a garlic press, cut the garlic in small pieces.) Add dry ingredients. Mix. Put ground beef, onion, and spice mixture in a dutch oven. Add tomato paste and two cans of water (12 ounces). Then, add beans and the two "bean cans" of water (30 ounces), for a total of 42 ounces of water. Cook over low heat at least 20-30 minutes.

Barbra Manning

JOHNNY MAZETTI

2 (7½ or 8½ ounce) packages
  broad egg noodles
1½ pounds ground chuck
1 large green bell pepper,
  chopped
2 medium onions, chopped
6 stalks celery, sliced
1½ teaspoons salt
1 teaspoon pepper
2 (6 ounce) cans buttom
  mushrooms

2 (8 ounce) cans tomato sauce
1 (10½ ounce) can cream of
  tomato soup
1 (8-10 ounce) bottle green
  olives, pitted, drained
1 (12 ounce) package sharp
  Cheddar cheese, cut into
  1 inch cubes

Cook noodles in salted water until barely tender. Do not over cook. Drain. Brown meat in oil. Remove meat and sauté pepper, onions and celery. Return meat to pan and add all remaining ingredients. Add noodles and mix well. Put into 9x13 baking dish. Bake at 350 degrees uncovered until bubbly.

Note: This freezes well. If frozen, thaw and cook as directed. Sliced ripe olives may be added. Yields 6-8 servings.

Jo Jones

MIKE'S CHILI

2 pounds ground chuck,
  browned and drained
1 medium red onion, chopped
½-¾ green bell pepper,
  chopped
1 clove garlic, minced
3 tablespoons olive oil
2 (16 ounce) cans kidney beans

2 (16 ounce) cans whole
  tomatoes
1 teaspoon pepper
1 teaspoon cumin
1 teaspoon sugar
2-3 tablespoons chili powder
salt to taste

Brown meat. In another pan, sauté onion, bell pepper, and garlic in olive oil. Add meat and all other ingredients and cook over simmering heat for 2 hours.

Libby Parks

HAMBURGER PIE

1 medium-sized onion, chopped
1 pound ground beef
Salt and pepper to taste
1 (17 ounce) can tender young
green peas
1 (10½ ounce) can condensed
tomato soup

5 medium-sized potatoes,
cooked
½ cup evaporated milk
2 tablespoons butter or
margarine

Brown onion in hot fat; add meat and seasonings; brown. Drain off excess fat. Add drained peas and soup; pour into a greased casserole. Mash potatoes; add milk and butter. Spoon in mounds over meat. Bake at 350 degrees for 30 minutes. Serves 6.

Catherine L. Pfeiffer

LASAGNA

1 clove garlic, minced
¾ cup onions, chopped
4 tablespoons olive oil
1 pound ground chuck
½ pound pork sausage
1 (28 ounce) can tomatoes
1 (15 ounce) can tomato sauce
2 tablespoons parsley, chopped
2 teaspoons sugar
1 teaspoon salt
½ teaspoon black pepper
½ teaspoon onion salt
1 teaspoon monosodium
glutamate

1½ teaspoons oregano, dried
1 dash hot pepper sauce
½ teaspoon basil leaves
½ teaspoon marjoram
½ teaspoon thyme
2 eggs
1 pound Ricotta cheese
1 (8 ounce) package lasagna
noodles, cooked
1½ cups Mozzarella cheese,
grated
1 cup Parmesan cheese, grated

In a large skillet, sauté onions and garlic in olive oil until lightly browned. Add ground chuck and pork sausage. Cook until meat loses its red color. Drain off all of the fat from the meat. In large saucepan, combine tomatoes, tomato sauce, parsley and all seasonings. Add the browned meat, onion, and garlic to the sauce. Simmer the entire mixture uncovered for one hour, stirring frequently as it thickens. Beat eggs slightly and mix with Ricotta cheese. Cook noodles until tender, drain and separate. Preheat oven to 350 degrees while assembling casserole. In bottom of large baking dish, place several spoonsfuls of tomato sauce (cover the bottom of the dish); then, alternately layer 5 lasagna noodles, tomato sauce, Ricotta and eggs mixture, Mozzarella and Parmesan cheese until all ingredients are used.

The top layer should be tomato sauce and grated cheeses. Bake in preheated oven for about 60 minutes, or until bubbly and brown. Remove from oven and let stand 15 minutes before serving. Serves 8 to 10.

Dianne Greenhill

MEAT LOAF

1½ pounds ground beef
1 cup cracker crumbs
1 (10½ ounce) can condensed
cream of tomato soup,
divided
2 stalks celery, chopped
1 egg
½ cup American cheese, cubed

1 large onion (2 inches in
diameter), chopped
½ green (bell) pepper, chopped
1½ teaspoons salt
¼ teaspoon pepper
American cheese slices
¼ cup water

Combine ground beef, cracker crumbs, ½ can tomato soup, celery, egg, cubed cheese, onion, green pepper, salt and pepper. Mix well and form into one large or two small loaves. Place in baking dish, top with American cheese slices. Combine water and remaining tomato soup and pour over cheese slices. Bake at 350 degrees for 45 minutes. Serves 8 to 10. (Loaves may be made a few days ahead, frozen, and baked when desired without thawing.)

Margaret Jenkins

GRANDMA'S MEAT LOAF

2 pounds ground beef or
ground chuck
12 ounces mild pork sausage
2 eggs, lightly beaten
2 tablespoons ketchup

1 tablespoon prepared mustard
¼ cup non fat dry milk solids
1 tablespoon onion flakes
¼ cup milk

Mix all ingredients (use your hand but, remove rings first). Put into large skillet or baking dish and shape into loaf. Add water to pan to one inch depth around meat loaf. Bake at 400 degrees for 1 hour or until top is crusty and brown. Serve with baked potato and tossed salad. Serves 6 to 8.

Pat Meade

LEMON BARBECUED MEAT LOAVES

1¼ pounds ground beef
4 slices day old bread, crusts removed
¼ cup lemon juice or lemon concentrate

¼ cup onion, minced
1 egg, slightly beaten
2 teaspoons seasoned salt

Combine meat, bread, lemon juice, onion, egg and seasoned salt, mix well. Form mixture into six individual loaves, place in baking dish so loaves touch but are not crowded. Bake in 350 degree oven for 15 minutes. Cover with sauce given below.

Sauce:
½ cup ketchup
⅓ cup light brown sugar
1 teaspoon dry mustard

¼ teaspoon ground allspice
¼ teaspoon ground cloves
6 thin lemon slices

Combine ketchup, sugar, mustard, allspice and cloves and pour over loaves. Bake 30 minutes longer. Put lemon slice on each loaf and bake 5 minutes longer. Serve with sauce. Instruct diners to squeeze lemon over meat.

Patricia D. Hallmark

LOW SODIUM - LOW CHOLESTEROL MEAT LOAF

¾ pound lean ground beef
2 tablespoons imitation eggs
2 tablespoons skim milk
1 slice low sodium bread, torn into small pieces

⅛ teaspoon red pepper
⅛ teaspoon garlic powder
⅛ teaspoon Italian seasoning
⅛ teaspoon parsley flakes
1 (10 ounce) can tomato puree

Mix ground beef, eggs, milk, bread and seasonings and mix thoroughly. Turn into lightly greased baking dish and shape into loaf. Bake in 350 degree oven for 35 minutes. Heat tomato puree to simmer, simmer at low heat for 30 minutes, stirring occasionally. Pour hot puree over meat loaf and bake 10 minutes longer. Serves 3.

The Committee

JOHNNY'S FAVORITE SPAGHETTI

1 pound ground beef
3 tablespoons olive oil
3 cloves garlic, minced
1 onion, chopped
1 (28 ounce) can tomatoes,
   chopped
1 (6 ounce) can tomato paste
1½ cups tomato juice
4 leaves basil, chopped, or
   2 teaspoons basil, dried

¼-½ teaspoon freshly ground
   black pepper
1 teaspoon salt
2 bay leaves
¼-½ cup red wine
½ cup Parmesan cheese
½ cup red wine

In a skillet, brown the beef. Drain off fat and set the beef aside. In a dutch oven, heat the olive oil over medium heat. Brown the garlic, add the onion and sauté until transparent. Add chopped tomatoes and tomato paste. Blend in the tomato juice, the basil, pepper, salt, bay leaves, ¼-½ cup red wine and the cooked beef. Simmer for 30-60 minutes over low heat stirring often. 15 minutes before serving, add cheese and remaining wine.

Tine Keller

SPAGHETTI SAUCE I

1 pound ground beef
1 cup onion, chopped
3 tablespoons olive oil
1 clove garlic, minced
3 (6 ounce) cans tomato paste
1 (28 ounce) can tomatoes

2 cups water
1 (2 ounce) jar mushrooms,
   sliced
1 teaspoon oregano
2 teaspoons salt
dash of pepper

Brown meat and onion in olive oil, drain and add minced garlic. Add all other ingredients, stir, and simmer uncovered for one hour. Serve over cooked spaghetti.

Carolyn Foster

SPAGHETTI SAUCE II

2 quarts tomatoes, drained
2 stalks celery, cut in 2″ pieces
1 teaspoon ground oregano
1 teaspoon salt

1 (3-4 ounce) cans tomato paste
Meat balls and/or Italian
    sausage (hot or mild)

Drain tomatoes (commercially canned or home canned) of the bulk of fluid. This will reduce your cooking time but be certain of the measure of tomatoes. Depending upon the amount of water in the canned tomatoes, you'll use 3-4 quarts to get this amount of tomatoes! Place tomatoes, celery, oregano and salt in the blender and liquify. In a sauce pan, bring to a boil and return to low heat for 2-2½ hours. After 30 minutes of low heat, add the tomato paste and stir well. Then, add your meat balls and/or Italian sausage. If using sausage, cut in your preference of serving pieces. Continue cooking for 2 hours. Cool over night in the refrigerator and remove the fat that has accumulated on the top of the sauce.

Note: This is an easy task for the evening before using it. It will freeze well. The flavor of the meat is retained but not the fat! You may delete the meat if desired. A bit of serendipity is the smell as it is cooking!

Shirley F. Burd

MEAT BALLS FOR SPAGHETTI SAUCE

2 eggs
1 teaspoon salt or salt
    substitute
¼ to ⅓ cup Romano cheese,
    grated (or Parmesan cheese)

¼ teaspoon ground oregano
1 pound ground beef
½ cup (approximately of stale
    bread, cubed or crumbs

Beat eggs well. Add to eggs, salt, cheese, and oregano. Mix in the ground beef. (The easiest way is to use your hands *without* your rings!) Add the cubed bread or bread crumbs and mix thoroughly. Add more bread crumbs if needed to form balls. Form into large or small balls, as you prefer. An ice-cream scoop (old fashioned metal kind) is useful for the large size. Cook meat balls in the spaghetti sauce for 1½ to 2 hours. (Ground beef has the best flavor if you follow the note in the spaghetti sauce to remove the fat after cooking.)

Shirley F. Burd

SPAGHETTI WITH MEAT SAUCE

3 tablespoons corn oil
3 pounds ground chuck
2 medium onions, peeled and
  minced
3 cloves garlic, peeled and
  minced
1 tablespoon Kitchen Bouquet
2 (28 ounce) cans tomatoes,
  diced
1 to 2 tablespoons salt
½ teaspoon pepper

½ teaspoon basil
2 (6 ounce) cans sliced
  mushrooms, drained
2 (6 ounce) cans tomato paste
1 (½ ounce) package Barzi
  spaghetti spices
3 packages (7 ounce) Vermicilli
  spaghetti, uncooked
1½ cups grated Parmesan
  cheese

Heat oil in large dutch oven. Cook beef until brown. Drain all fat. Add onions, garlic, Kitchen Bouquet, and tomatoes with their juice, stir well. Add all remaining ingredients, except spaghetti and cheese. Bring to a boil. Lower heat and simmer for 1 hour. (May simmer covered or uncovered. Covered usually makes it more flavorful.) Cook spaghetti according to directions on package. Drain. Add one tablespoon of corn oil and toss spaghetti to spread oil evenly. This prevents sticking. Top spaghetti with the sauce. Sprinkle top with cheese. Makes 12 servings.

Mary L. Shannon

SWEDISH MEAT BALLS

2 pounds ground beef
½ cup onion, minced
¾ cup bread crumbs
1 tablespoon parsley, snipped
2 teaspoons salt
dash pepper

1 teaspoon Worcestershire
  sauce
1 egg
½ cup milk
¼ cup salad oil

Mix thoroughly beef, onion, bread crumbs, parsley, salt, pepper, Worchestershire sauce, egg and milk. Refrigerate 2 hours. Shape into · bite-size balls. In large skillet slowly brown and cook meatballs in oil. Remove and keep warm. Use same skillet to make sauce.

Sauce:
½ cup flour
1 teaspoon paprika
½ teaspoon salt

dash pepper
2 cups water
1 cup sour cream

Blend flour, paprika, salt and pepper into skillet and cook over low heat, stirring until mixture is smooth and bubbly (it does not have to brown). Stir in water and heat to boiling, stirring constantly. Boil one minute and reduce heat. Add sour cream and mix until smooth. Add meatballs and serve as hot main dish. Serves large party as hot hors de oeuvres.

Nell Pewitt

CORN DOGS

1 cup self-rising flour
2 tablespoons sugar
⅔ cup corn meal
2 tablespoons shortening,
  melted

1 egg
¾ cup milk
1 pound hot dogs

Mix flour, sugar and meal; add shortening and blend well. Add eggs and mix well. Add milk and mix well. Batter should be very thick. Roll hot dogs in batter and fry in deep fat.

Note: Hot dogs should not be frozen, it is best to have the hot dogs at room temperature before rolling in batter.

Donna Thompson

EASY PORK CHOP CASSEROLE

2 cups water
1 cup rice, uncooked
1 (3⅛ ounce) package onion
   soup mix

6 pork chops

Preheat oven to 350 degrees. Mix water, rice and soup mix. Put into large baking dish and arrange pork chops on top. Cover with foil and bake for 1½ hours.

Pat Worley

PINEAPPLE AND HONEY-GLAZED KABOBS

1 pound American Dinner
   sausage (John Morrell)
1 (1 pound, 4 ounce) can
   pineapple chunks, drained,
   (reserve juice)

1 medium zucchini, cut into ¼
   inch slices
½ cup honey
⅛ teaspoon ginger
½ cup reserved pineapple juice

Cut sausage into bite-sized chunks. Arrange sausage, pineapple chunks, and zucchini slices alternately on four 8 inch skewers. Combine honey, ginger and pineapple juice in a small saucepan. Bring to a boil, reduce heat and simmer 5-10 minutes. Broil or grill skewered meat and vegetables 8-10 minutes, turning and basting frequently with honey and juice mixture Serves 4.

Patricia D. Hallmark

EASY CROCK POT PORK ROAST

3-4 pound boneless pork roast
2-3 cups water
3 tablespoons Worcestershire
   sauce

2 bay leaves
salt and pepper to taste

Put roast into crockpot. Add water, Worcestershire sauce and spices. Cover and cook on the high setting overnight. Reduce crockpot to the low setting and cook for 8 more hours. Serves 4.

Note: Good to put on before bed, reduce heat in the morning and it will be done when you come home from work.

Barbra Manning

NEW ORLEANS RED BEANS AND RICE WITH HAM

3 large onions, chopped
    coarsely
3 tablespoons bacon drippings
1¼ cups water
salt and pepper to taste
5 shakes of hot pepper sauce
3 to 4 shakes of Worcestershire
    sauce

2 cloves garlic, chopped
3 teaspoons dried parsley
3 (15 ounce) cans of Van
    Camp's New Orleans Style
    Red Kidney Beans
2 cups cooked ham, chopped
2½ cups water

In a large dutch oven or iron pan, sauté onions in bacon drippings; add water, salt, pepper, pepper sauce, Worcestershire sauce, garlic, and parsley. Add beans, ham, and water. Simmer for 1 hour on medium low heat. Serve over rice. Serves 6 to 8.

Mary Pat Van Epps

BARBECUED RIBS

ribs for barbecuing
barbecue sauce

seasonings as desired
1 baking bag

Preheat oven to 350 degrees. Place desired number of ribs in large cooking bag. Add generous amount of barbecue sauce and any other seasonings as desired. Seal bag and pierce several times. Bake for one hour. Remove from bag. Baste and brown.

Margaret Jenkins

SAUSAGE CASSEROLE

1 pound hot sausage
1 pound mild sausage
5 green onions, chopped
5 ribs celery, chopped
1 bell pepper, chopped
1 (4 ounce) package slivered
   almonds

2 (6 ounce) cans mushrooms
2 cups rice, cooked
2 (3¾ ounce) packages chicken
   noodle soup mix
½ cup water
½ cup buttered bread crumbs

Fry hot and mild sausage, drain and crumble. Sauté in the drippings the onions, celery and bell pepper until clear. Drain and add to sausage. Then add almonds, mushrooms, rice and chicken noodle soup with water. Combine in casserole and cover with buttered bread crumbs. Bake for 45 minutes in a 350 degree oven.

Margaret Jenkins

PATTY CARBOTTI'S SAUSAGE DISH

1 pound bulk sausage
   (hot style is best)
2 stalks celery, chopped
1 medium onion, peeled and
   chopped
2 carrots, chopped

1 envelope dry noodle soup mix
1 can water chestnuts, drained
   and quartered
1 cup rice, uncooked
2 cups water

In a skillet, brown sausage; drain. Add celery, onion, carrots; cook until soft. Add envelope of soup and mix well with sausage and vegetables. Add chestnuts, rice and water. Cook over low heat, covered, until rice is cooked. Serves 4-5.

Note: This can easily be cooked in an electric skillet to save energy. Recipe can be extended by adding more rice and/or vegetables. Very good warmed over!

Patricia D. Hallmark

TOAD IN THE HOLE

1 pound small link pork
  sausage
1 cup milk
2 eggs
1 cup all purpose flour

½ teaspoon salt
⅛ teaspoon black pepper,
  freshly ground
1 tablespoon butter, melted

Fry sausage until lightly browned and all fat has been rendered. Place sausages, evenly arranged, in 9 inch square baking dish. Place remaining ingredients in blender and blend for one minute until smooth. Pour batter over sausages and bake uncovered in a 400 degree oven for 30 minutes. The batter will become puffy, crisp and brown. Serves 4.

Mary Jane Dishion

VEAL AND PEPPERS

¾ pound boneless veal
2 tablespoons oil
2 green peppers, cut into 12
  strips each
1 (3-4 ounce) can mushrooms,
  any cut

1 (8 ounce) can tomato sauce
½ pinch red pepper, crushed
dash red pepper sauce, optional
salt and pepper to taste

Cut meat into bite-size pieces. This is easier if the veal is partially frozen. Heat oil and brown meat on all sides. Add green pepper strips and cover. Cook for 8-9 minutes, stirring often. Add undrained mushrooms, tomato sauce, red pepper and pepper sauce (optional). Simmer 20-30 minutes and season with salt and pepper to taste. Serve with salad, rolls and a dry white wine if you wish. Serves 2. (This can be doubled or tripled with ease; it can be prepared ahead of time—holding the simmering until just before serving. Allow for re-heating time.)

Shirley F. Burd

Poultry and Game

BAKED CHICKEN

6-8 chicken breasts   **1 cup heavy cream**
¼ cup flour   **Seasoning salt**

Flour chicken and sprinkle heavily with seasoning salt. Pour cream over chicken and bake in a two quart casserole with a tight fitting cover at 350 degrees for 50 minutes. Uncover and bake 15 minutes longer.

Catherine Robertson

BONJOUR POULET

**1 (8 ounce) package herb
  seasoned stuffing mix**
½ cup butter, melted
1 cup chicken broth
**2½ cups chicken, cooked and
  chopped**
½ cup celery, chopped

**¼ cup chives or green onion
  tops, chopped**
½ cup parsley, chopped
½ cup mayonnaise
**1 (10¾ ounce) can mushroom
  soup, undiluted**
Cheddar cheese, grated

Combine stuffing mix, butter and broth. Spread ½ of the stuffing mix over the bottom of a 9x13 baking dish. Mix together the chicken, celery, chives, (onion tops) parsley and mayonnaise and pour into baking dish over the stuffing. Top with remaining stuffing mixture, cover and refrigerate overnight. (Will keep 2-3 days, if desired). Remove from refrigerator and allow to sit at room temperature for 1 hour. Spread soup over top of stuffing and bake at 325 degrees for 40 minutes. Remove from oven, sprinkle with cheese and bake for 10 minutes more. Serves 8.

Armantine Keller

CHERRY CHICKEN

salt
pepper
garlic powder
6 chicken breasts
¼ cup butter
½ cup dry vermouth

2 small jars cherry preserves
1 (6 ounce) can frozen orange
  juice
1 can mandarin oranges,
  drained
1 can pitted cherries, drained

Put salt, pepper and garlic powder on the chicken breasts; cover and refrigerate for several hours. About 2 hours before serving time, put butter, vermouth, cherry preserves, and frozen orange juice in a sauce pan. Heat to boiling; then simmer for 15 minutes. Arrange chicken breasts in a baking dish, skin side down and pour sauce over it. Bake at 350 degrees for 45 minutes. Turn chicken skin side up and bake another 45 minutes, basting every 15 minutes. Add mandarin oranges and pitted cherries. Serves 6.

Brenda Y. Smith

CHICKEN PARMIGIANA

3 chicken breasts (about 12
  ounces each) split, skinned
  and boned
2 eggs, lightly beaten
1 teaspoon salt
⅛ teaspoon pepper
¾ cup fine dry bread crumbs
½ cup vegetable oil

2 (8 ounce) cans tomato sauce
¼ teaspoon basil leaf
⅛ teaspoon garlic powder or
  minced garlic
1 tablespoon margarine
½ cup Parmesan cheese
8 ounces Mozzarella cheese,
  sliced and cut into triangles

Place chicken breasts on cutting board and pound lightly with side of knife or cleaver until about ¼ inch thick. Combine eggs, salt and pepper. Dip chicken in egg mixture, then in bread crumbs. Heat oil in large skillet until very hot, quickly brown chicken on both sides and remove to shallow baking dish. Pour excess oil from skillet. Pour tomato sauce, basil and garlic in skillet, stir and bring to boil. Reduce heat and simmer for ten minutes or until mixture thickens, stir in margarine until it melts. Pour over chicken, sprinkle with Parmesan cheese, cover with foil and bake at 350 degrees for 30 minutes. Remove cover, place Mozzarella cheese over chicken and bake ten minutes longer or until cheese melts. Makes 6 servings.

Kathy Mahew

CHICKEN-SOUR CREAM

6 chicken breasts, or fryer
  pieces
1 teaspoon salt
⅛ teaspoon pepper
2 tablespoons butter

1 (4 ounce) package Roquefort
  cheese
1 garlic clove, minced
1 cup sour cream

Season chicken with salt and pepper; brown in butter. Place chicken in casserole dish and set aside. Mix the chicken drippings with cheese, garlic and sour cream. Heat and pour over the chicken. Cover the casserole and bake at 350 degrees for 1 hour. Serves 6.

Margaret Jenkins

ALPINE CHICKEN CASSEROLE

4 cups chicken, cooked and
  chopped
2 cups celery, sliced
2 cups bread cubes, toasted
1 cup salad dressing
½ cup milk

¼ cup onion, chopped
1 teaspoon salt
dash of pepper
1 (8 ounce) package Swiss
  cheese, cut in thin strips
¼ cup toasted slivered almonds

Preheat oven to 350 degrees. Combine ingredients except almonds; mix well. Pour into 2½ quart baking dish; sprinkle with nuts. Bake for 30 to 40 minutes. Serves 6.

Note: Casserole may be made ahead; covered and refrigerated for several hours. Do not preheat oven if casserole has been refrigerated. Bake covered for 50 minutes. Remove cover; continue baking for 10 minutes.

Leon S. McAulay

HOT CHICKEN CASSEROLE

4 cups chicken, cooked, cooled
and cubed
2 tablespoons lemon juice
⅔ cup almonds, chopped
¾ cup mayonnaise
1 teaspoon salt
2 cups celery, chopped

4 eggs, hard boiled and sliced
1 (10½ ounce) can cream of
chicken soup
1 teaspoon onion, minced
2 pimientos, minced
1½ cups potato chips, crushed
1 cup cheese, grated

Combine all ingredients, except cheese and chips. Place in large casserole. Top with cheese and chips. Let stand overnight in refrigerator. Bake at 400 degrees for 20-25 minutes. Serves 8.

Cindy Hinds

CHICKEN AND BEEF CASSEROLE

1 (4 ounce) jar dried beef
6 or 8 chicken breasts, boned
and skinned
6 or 8 slices bacon
1 (4 ounce) can mushrooms,
drained

1 (2¾ ounce) package slivered
almonds
1 (10¾ ounce) can cream of
mushroom soup
1 (8 ounce) carton sour cream

Line large casserole or 9x13 inch baking dish with dried beef. Roll chicken breasts in bacon slices and secure with toothpicks; place in the casserole dish. Add mushrooms and almonds. Mix undiluted soup and sour cream. Pour over chicken. Cook in a 250 degree oven for 3 hours or until tender. Serves 6 to 8.

Margaret Jenkins

CHICKEN CORN CASSEROLE

⅓ cup butter
⅓ cup flour
1 cup chicken broth, hot
1 cup milk
1½ teaspoons salt
½ teaspoon pepper

1 tablespoon onion, finely
  chopped
2 cups chicken, chopped
1 (12 ounce) can mexicorn
½ cup sharp cheese, grated
buttered bread crumbs

Preheat oven to 350 degrees. Melt butter and blend into flour. Stir in broth and milk. Stir constantly until thick. Add salt, pepper and onion. Combine this sauce with the chicken, corn, and cheese. Pour into casserole, top with buttered cracker or bread crumbs. Bake 25 minutes. Serves 6.

Cyndy Inman

CHICKEN AND WILD RICE CASSEROLE

1 (7 ounce) package long grain
  and wild rice
1 (10½ ounce) can cream of
  celery soup

1 (10½ ounce) can chicken and
  rice soup
1 cup milk
6 chicken breasts

Sprinkle uncooked rice evenly over bottom of a greased 8x13 inch baking dish. In a sauce pan combine soups and milk, mix well and heat. Pour soup mixture carefully over rice, arrange chicken breasts on top. Cover dish with foil to seal. Bake at 325 degrees for 2 hours. Serves 6.

Note: Converted rice may be used instead of long grain and wild rice. Use 1 cup converted rice and 1 (1 ounce) package onion soup mix.

Nell Pewitt

CHICKEN ADOBO

½ cup vinegar
½ cup soy sauce
2 cups water
2 bay leaves
1 teaspoon salt

¼ teaspoon pepper
1 whole chicken, cut up, or 6 to
  8 chicken breasts
1 to 2 teaspoons minced garlic

Mix vinegar, soy sauce, water, bay leaves, salt and pepper in large pot or dutch oven. Bring mixture to boil. Add chicken. Sprinkle minced garlic powder over chicken, cover and reduce heat to medium (slow boil). Cook until chicken is done—about 30 to 45 minutes. Serves 4 to 6.

Barbra Manning

CHICKEN CACCIATORE

1 (3 pound) frying chicken, cut up
2 tablespoons cooking oil
1 medium clove garlic, minced
1 teaspoon oregano, crumbled
1 teaspoon salt
¼ teaspoon pepper
1 cup mushrooms, sliced
1 (1 pound) can tomatoes

Brown chicken pieces in oil and garlic. Before turning, sprinkle the chicken with oregano, salt and pepper. Add mushrooms and brown lightly. Add the stewed tomatoes; cover and simmer for 30 minutes or until chicken is tender. Delicious over rice. Serves 4.

Willie Mae Gary

CHICKEN CURRY

½ cup fat
2 cups onion, chopped
½ cup green bell pepper, · chopped
1 frying chicken, cut up
2 tablespoons flour
½ tablespoon curry powder
1½ teaspoons salt
½ cup water
¼ cup lemon juice
1 (8 ounce) can tomato sauce
2 cloves garlic, crushed
1 (6 ounce) can mushrooms, drained

Melt fat; add onions and bell pepper; cook until tender. Add chicken; fry until browned. Mix together the flour, curry powder and salt; slowly stir in water and lemon juice to make a paste. Add tomato sauce and garlic; pour over chicken. Add mushrooms. Cover. Simmer over low heat until tender, about 2 hours. Serve with wild or white rice. Serves 4 to 6.

Margaret Jenkins

CHICKEN DIVAN I

½ cup bread crumbs
½ cup butter, melted
2 whole chicken breasts

2 (10 ounce) packages frozen
   broccoli

Sauce:
1 (10½ ounce) can cream of
   chicken soup, undiluted
½ cup mayonnaise
2 teaspoons dry mustard

¼ cup dry sherry
1 teaspoon salt
½ teaspoon pepper

Topping:
¼ cup bread crumbs
½ cup sharp Cheddar cheese,
   grated

¼ cup almonds, sliced

Line 6x10 inch casserole dish with bread crumbs; pour ¾ of melted butter over crumbs. Boil chicken breasts for 30 minutes; then cool, debone and cut into bite size pieces. Cook broccoli according to package directions; then drain, cool and separate into stalks. Combine sauce ingredients and mix thoroughly. Place layer of cooked broccoli on top of bread crumbs and melted butter; layer cooked chicken pieces on top of broccoli; pour sauce over chicken layer and shake it down through layers. Preheat oven to 400 degrees. Sprinkle bread crumbs, grated cheese and almonds over the top and pour the rest of the melted butter over the topping. Bake for 30 minutes. Serves 4 to 6.

Shirley Colson

DICK'S HONEYED CHICKEN BREASTS

4 chicken breasts, boned and
   skinless
½ cup orange juice
salt to taste
pepper to taste

bread crumbs
½ cup butter, melted
½ cup honey
½ cup white wine

Bone and remove skin of chicken breasts. Dip chicken into the orange juice. Add salt and pepper to bread crumbs. Coat chicken with crumbs. Arrange in a casserole or baking pan in a single layer. Bake for 40 minutes at 325 degrees starting with a cold oven. Combine melted butter, honey and wine. Pour over chicken and bake for 30 minutes more. Serves 4.

Florence Hansen

CHICKEN DIVAN II

1 (10 ounce) package frozen
  chopped broccoli
1 (8 ounce) package cream
  cheese, room temperature
1 cup milk
½ teaspoon garlic salt

½ teaspoon salt
¾ cup Parmesan cheese
1¼ pounds chicken, cooked
  and boned
½ cup Parmesan cheese

Cook broccoli until almost tender; drain well. In double boiler, blend cream cheese, milk, seasonings and Parmesan cheese and cook until cheese is melted. Grease 1½ quart casserole dish and line with broccoli. Pour ½ of hot cheese mixture over broccoli. Arrange chicken pieces over cheese and add remaining cheese mixture. Sprinkle ½ cup Parmesan cheese over the top. Bake for 30 minutes in a 350 degree oven. Serves 6 to 8.

Sherry Wilson

CHICKEN RICE FIESTA

½ cup celery, diced
4-6 green onions, chopped
½ cup margarine
½ cup green pepper, chopped
1 cup rice, uncooked
2 tablespoons pimiento,
  chopped
½ cup mushrooms, sliced or
  chopped

1 (10¾ ounce) can cream of
  chicken soup
1 (10¾ ounce) can cream of
  celery soup
1 can water chestnuts, sliced
½ cup chicken broth
3 cups cooked chicken, diced

Sauté celery, onion, and pepper in margarine. Combine with all other ingredients and bake in a covered 2-quart casserole for 1½ hours at 275 degrees.

Note: Lightly butter the casserole lid around the edge before placing on dish, will prevent sticking. Serves 8-12.

Carolyn Foster

CHICKEN MARINADE

5-6 chicken breasts or whole
   chicken, cut up
1 egg, beaten
1 cup oil
1 cup vinegar

1½ teaspoons poultry
   seasoning
1 tablespoon salt
1 dash pepper

Wash chicken and remove skin. Mix all ingredients and marinate chicken in mixture in refrigerator over night, or 4-8 hours. Grill slowly, basting chicken with marinade as it cooks. Cook until meat comes loose from bone. Tastes great.

Dawn Ward

CHICKEN PAPRIKA

4 tablespoons butter or oil
1 medium onion, chopped
¾ cup water
1 (3-4 pound) chicken, cut
   serving size
1 green bell pepper, chopped

1 tomato, seeded and chopped
salt and pepper to taste
1 tablespoon hot Hungarian
   paprika
1 cup sour cream, commercial
   type

In a large skillet or dutch oven, heat the butter (oil). Add the chopped onion and sauté over moderate heat for 1-3 minutes. Add ½ to ¾ cup of the water. Put lid on and reduce the heat to the lowest possible temperature; simmer for ¾ to 1 hour to gain the maximum flavor from the onion. Watch occasionally to see that it doesn't go dry. Add the green pepper, tomato, salt, pepper and paprika. Mix well. Add the cut up chicken. Cover and cook for 45 minutes at moderate temperature or until chicken is tender. Remove chicken to a warmed platter and cover. Add the sour cream to the remainder, placing the heat down to simmer or turn the stove off. All that is wanted is to warm the gravy with the cream thoroughly. Pour the gravy over the chicken. Serves 4. Serve with a green vegetable, mashed potatoes or rice, roll and a salad.

Shirley F. Burd

SWEET AND SOUR CHICKEN

6 chicken breasts, skinned
½ cup margarine
1 cup celery, chopped

1 clove garlic, minced
1 (46 ounce) can sweetened
   orange juice

Using an electric skillet, braise chicken breasts in margarine. Add celery and garlic. Add orange juice until skillet is ⅔ full. Cook for 3 hours at 250 degrees or sufficient heat to keep the juice bubbling. As the fluid reduces, add the remaining juice until the entire can is used. The meat and gravy will be golden brown. Serve over rice. Serves 6.

Mary L. Morris

HOT BROWNS (SANDWICH)

6 slices Russian Rye bread
6 slices turkey breast
4 tablespoons butter
4 tablespoons flour
2 cups milk

3 cups mild Cheddar cheese,
   grated
12 slices bacon, cooked and
   crumbled
½ cup Parmesan cheese, grated

Toast bread; layer thick turkey slices on top of bread. Melt butter in double boiler; add flour and mix to a smooth paste. Add milk and stir until thick. Add grated cheese and stir until melted and blended. Place open-face sandwiches in a low sided pan and pour ⅓ cup cheese sauce over each. Top with crumbled bacon and grated Parmesan cheese. Broil until cheese begins to bubble and serve hot. Serves 6.

Shirley Colson

VENISON

steaks
chops

roast

Soak meat in cold salted water (1 tablespoon salt to 1 quart water) for at least 2 hours. Roasts and frozen cuts should soak overnight. This removes the "gamey" taste. Dry meat and treat with Adolph's Meat Tenderizer as instructed for cut of meat. Cook meat as you would a similar cut of beef. The salt water soaks will render any wild game meat tasty.

Pat Meade

ROAST DOVE

1 tablespoon butter per dove
1 teaspoon tarragon per
  6 doves
1 teaspoon thyme per 6 doves
½ teaspoon garlic powder per
  6 doves

pepper to taste per 6 doves
wild doves, dressed
1 green onion per dove
½ slice bacon per dove
1 piece string 8-10″ long per
  dove

Mix butter and spices together. Stuff cavity of each dove with approximately 1 tablespoon butter mixture. Wash green onions and cut so their length equals length of dove. Place onion in middle of stuffing. Wrap each dove with bacon slice and tie with string. Place breast side down on broiler pan. Preheat oven to 350 degrees. Bake for 30-35 minutes until bacon begins to brown. (Note: increase spices as number of birds increases). 6 wild doves serve 2.

Pat Hickman

PILAF OF QUAIL WITH RAISINS

5 tablespoons butter, divided
1 tablespoon vegetable oil
4-6 quail (wild)
onions, ½ cup finely chopped
1 tablespoon garlic, finely
  chopped

1½ cups long grain rice
3 cups cold water
½ cup raisins
1 pinch salt
1 pinch pepper

Wash quail. Melt 2 tablespoons of the butter in large 3-4 quart casserole. Add oil. Brown birds turning until browned evenly. Remove birds and set aside. Add remaining 3 tablespoons butter. Add onions and garlic. Fry approximately 5 minutes, stirring frequently. When onions soften and become golden, pour in rice and stir for 2-3 minutes. Mix in water, raisins, pinch of salt and pepper. Bring to boil over high heat. Arrange quail on top of rice. Cover casserole tightly and bake in middle of oven at 350 degrees for 15-20 minutes, or until liquid is absorbed by rice. To test quail for doneness, pierce thigh with sharp knife. If juice is a pale yellow with no trace of pink, they're done. If not, cook 5-10 minutes. Serves 4.

Pat Hickman

Fish and Seafood

CLAM SAUCE FOR SPINACH SPAGHETTI

2-3 tablespoons cooking oil
1 tablespoon dried parsley
2 tablespoons dried chives
1 small onion (1 inch in
　diameter), chopped

3 cloves garlic, minced
1 (8 ounce) can minced clams,
　undrained
¾ cup water

Sauté in oil the parsley, chives, onion and garlic until the onions are golden brown. Add the undrained clams and water. Simmer 30 to 40 minutes. Serve on prepared spinach spaghetti (the green variety) with garlic bread, a salad, and your preference of a dry white wine.

Note: After you make this sauce once, you can estimate the amount of fresh chives and parsley to be used by appearance.

Shirley F. Burd

SEAFOOD GUMBO

1 pound okra, sliced thin
1 pound can of tomatoes
1 medium onion, chopped
½ green bell pepper, diced
1 stalk celery, chopped
1 clove garlic, minced
salt and pepper to taste
¾ cup butter
¾ cup flour

1 small bunch green onions,
　chopped (separate white and
　green parts)
hot water
2 pounds fresh shrimp
　(shelled, if you wish)
3 cooked crabs (in pieces in
　shells to be authentic)

Combine okra, tomatoes, onion, green bell pepper, celery, garlic, salt and pepper in a skillet and cook until quite soft, about 1-2 hours. In a large pot, make a dark roux with the butter and flour. Add the white part of the onions to roux and cook slightly. Add hot water to roux until it becomes the consistency of cream. Add to roux, the shrimp and crabs. You may want to add oysters, but they take longer to cook. Now, add the okra mixture and other seasonings you like such as parsley, Worcestershire sauce, hot sauce, etc. Cook until shrimp are done and flavors are blended. Add the chopped green onion tops and cook five minutes more. Serve over rice and sprinkle with filé powder as desired.

Linda White

SHRIMP AND OKRA GUMBO

2 cups fresh okra, diced
2 tablespoons oil
½ cup margarine
4 tablespoons flour
1 onion
1 bell pepper
2 stalks celery
1 tablespoon scallions,
  chopped

2 cloves garlic
3 quarts water
1 tablespoon Worcestershire
  sauce
2 pounds fresh shrimp, peeled
boiled rice

In a heavy aluminum dutch oven, fry okra in 2 tablespoons oil for 10 minutes, stirring constantly as not to burn. Remove okra and set aside. Add margarine and flour making a roux in the same pot. Cook roux until chocolate brown, stirring constantly. Chop all vegetables and garlic and add them and the okra. Cook on low for 5 minutes. Add water and Worcestershire sauce and cook on low for 1-2 hours. Add shrimp and cook on low for 30 minutes. Serve over boiled rice and garnish with chopped scallions.

Hilda Stansbury

SAUTÉED LOBSTER

Rock lobster tails (3 tails per
  person) or whole lobster
1 tablespoon salt per quart of
  water

¼-½ pound of butter
  (not margarine)

Boil lobster or lobster tails in salted water for 4-8 minutes. Cool. Remove meat from the shell. Cut into bite size pieces. Reserve in a covered dish and refrigerate. When ready to prepare dinner, sauté in butter until hot. Serve with hot rolls, a tossed salad, a broccoli souffle and a Chablis wine.

Shirley F. Burd

BAKED MACKEREL

4 pounds mackerel
butter

salt and pepper to taste
Hollandaise Sauce

Preheat oven to 400 degrees. Clean the mackerel. Oil an oval baking dish or pan. Place fish in dish or pan. Dot with butter. Sprinkle with salt and pepper. Bake for 50-60 minutes, basting with drippings. Serve with Hollandaise sauce. Serves 4-6 people.

Shirley F. Burd

OYSTER STEW

1 pint oysters, fresh or canned
1 quart milk
2 tablespoons butter

salt, pepper and cayenne
pepper to taste

Simmer oysters in their liquor until the edges of the oysters begin to curl. In another pan, heat milk almost to the boiling point. Add butter and seasonings to the oysters. Add the scalded milk to the oysters. Serve with hot bread fresh out of the oven. May use OTC Trenton Oyster crackers in place of hot bread. Serves two.

Note: Should oysters be a favorite, increase amount up to one quart for a very hearty stew. I often add the seasoning at the end and recommend this for all using the recipe for the first time.

Shirley F. Burd

SALMON PATTIES

1 (16 ounce) can salmon,
   undrained
1 cup flour

1 cup corn meal
2 eggs, slightly beaten
cooking oil

Thoroughly mix all ingredients except cooking oil. Pour oil into skillet to ¼ inch depth. Let skillet and oil get very hot. Spoon salmon mixture into oil with a tablespoon. Brown on both sides.

Note: May add grated onion to mixture before cooking if desired.

Tom Proctor

VEGETABLE BALLS WITH SCALLOPS

1 pound radishes
1 pound carrots
½ pound scallops
6 cups vegetable oil
4 cups soup stock

1 teaspoon salt
1 teaspoon monosodium
  glutamate
1 tablespoon cornstarch

Remove skin of radishes and carrots. Cut carrots and trim carrots and radishes into small balls. (Carrots can be cut into ½-⅔ inch pieces, but are prettier if carved into balls.) Boil scallops and shred. Soak the radish and carrot balls in hot oil (425 degrees) for 5 minutes, remove and drain excess oil. Heat 3 tablespoons oil, add soup stock and vegetable balls. Cover and cook over medium heat for 25 minutes. Remove balls and put on serving plate. Boil soup with salt, MSG and scallops. Add cornstarch and one tablespoon oil. Mix well and pour over vegetable balls and serve.

Ann Chen

TUNA NOODLE CASSEROLE

1 (12 ounce) package sea shell
  noodles
2 slices bacon
½ large bell pepper, chopped
½ medium onion, chopped

1 (6½ ounce) can tuna
1 (10¾ ounce) can cream of
  mushroom soup
1 soup can of milk
½ cup bread crumbs

Follow package directions for cooking noodles. While noodles are cooking, fry bacon in a large skillet. Remove bacon when moderately crisp and save. Sauté bell pepper and onion in bacon fat until onion is golden brown. Add tuna, soup and milk and mix well. When noodles are done, drain well and add to skillet mixture. Simmer uncovered 20 to 30 minutes or until thickened, stirring frequently. Pour into a casserole dish, top with crumbled bacon and bread crumbs. Place under broiler until bread crumbs are toasted. Serves 4.

Note: A mild cheese, grated, may be added to bread crumb topping or used in its stead.

Martha C. Yancey

STIR FRIED SHRIMP AND CHICKEN MEAT WITH CASHEWS

9 ounces chicken meat, diced
1 egg white, divided
3 teaspoons cornstarch, divided
7 ounces shrimp
½ bamboo shoot
¼ carrot
½ green pepper
1 teaspoon salt
1 teaspoon sugar
½ teaspoon monosodium
   glutamate

dash black pepper
1 teaspoon sesame oil
1 tablespoon water
6 cups vegetable oil
1 scallion, chopped
1 slice ginger root
1 teaspoon sherry
6 ounces cashews

Dice chicken, marinate with ½ egg white and 1 teaspoon cornstarch. Mix cleaned shrimp with ½ egg white and 1 teaspoon cornstarch. Cut bamboo shoot, carrot, and green pepper into diamond shape (sliced diagonally). Mix salt, sugar, MSG, pepper, sesame oil, remaining cornstarch and water, stir well and reserve. Heat 6 cups oil (375 degrees) and deep fry shrimp, chicken, bamboo shoot, green pepper and carrot until tender, then remove. Stir fry 1 chopped scallion and ginger root in 1 tablespoon oil and add meat and vegetables. Add sherry and reserved seasonings and cashews. Stir fry quickly over high heat and serve at once.

Note: Ginger root is usually discarded, as its flavor is very strong.

Ann Chen

Eggs and Cheese

BACON AND CHEESE OVEN OMELET

12 slices bacon
6 slices American cheese

8 eggs, beaten
1 cup milk

Cook bacon until crisp. Drain. Crumble 4 slices and leave others whole. Cut cheese slices into halves; arrange in the bottom of a lightly buttered 9 inch pan. Beat together eggs and milk with a fork, rotary beater or electric mixer at low speed for 4-5 minutes. Add crumbled bacon. Pour over cheese. Bake for 30 minutes in a pre-heated 350 degree oven. Arrange whole bacon slices on top of omelet as spokes in a wheel. Bake 10 minutes longer. Let stand 5 minutes before cutting.

Note: This recipe can easily be doubled and baked in a 9x13 inch pan. Bacon can be prepared a day ahead, wrapped in plastic wrap and refrigerated.

Roberta Dalpini

BRUNCH EGGS

½ cup butter
18 eggs, beaten
½-¾ cup milk
1 teaspoon salt
½ teaspoon pepper
4 dashes hot pepper sauce, or to taste
1 (10¾ ounce) can cream of mushroom soup

1 medium onion, chopped fine
¼ cup green pepper, chopped fine (optional)
1 (6 ounce) jar mushrooms or ½ cup fresh, chopped
¼ cup sherry
1 cup Cheddar cheese, grated
¼ cup Cheddar cheese, grated

Melt butter in large skillet. Combine eggs, milk, salt, pepper and hot pepper sauce and pour into skillet. Cook until just set. Transfer to a 9x13 inch casserole dish. Combine soup, onion, pepper, mushrooms, sherry and 1 cup of cheese and pour over eggs. Sprinkle with remaining ¼ cup cheese. Cover and refrigerate overnight. Bring to room temperature and bake at 350 degrees for 30 minutes or until set. Serves 12-15. Delicious served with sliced baked ham.

Tine Keller

EGG AND CRABMEAT CASSEROLE

½ cup butter
18 eggs, beaten
½ cup half and half
salt
pepper
4-5 dashes hot pepper sauce
1 (10¾ ounce) can cream of
   mushroom soup

¼ cup sherry
1 cup fresh mushrooms, sliced
1½ cups Swiss cheese, grated
2 (6 ounce) cans lump crab
   meat or 1 (10 ounce) frozen
   package
6-8 green onions, chopped fine

Melt butter in a large skillet. Combine eggs, half and half, salt, pepper and hot pepper sauce. Pour into skillet and cook until just set. Mix together with remaining ingredients. Transfer to a 9x13 inch casserole dish. Cover and refrigerate over night. Bring to room temperature and bake at 350 degrees for 30-45 minutes or until set. Serves 12-15.

Tine Keller

SCOTCH EGGS

A good finger food for picnics or traveling if left whole or split them in half, length ways for hors' D'oeuvres or eat them with a salad for lunch.

6 eggs, hard-boiled
½ cup flour
½ pound sausage meat (bulk)

1 egg, beaten
seasoned bread crumbs
oil for deep frying

Hard-boil the eggs, cool and peel. Lightly dust eggs with flour. Divide sausage into 6 portions. Wrap each egg in a portion of the sausage meat (it's easier to flatten the portion, curving it slightly, insert the egg and roll between the hands.) Make sure that all of the egg is covered with approximately the same thickness of sausage. Dip the sausage covered egg in the beaten egg and roll in the bread crumbs. Deep fry in oil until lightly browned. Two or three may be done at the same time as long as the oil continues to boil. Drain and cool on paper towels. To be eaten cold. Split if used for hors' D'oeuvres.

Brenda Coulehan

CHEESE GRITS SOUFFLÉ

½ cup grits
2 cups boiling water
½ teaspoon salt
½ cup sharp Cheddar cheese,
    grated

1 cup milk
3 eggs, well-beaten
¾ teaspoon salt

Cook grits as directed on package in boiling water and salt. Add grated cheese and allow to cool. Stir in milk, eggs, and salt and beat until smooth. Pour into a buttered baking dish and bake 30-45 minutes at 375 degrees. Serves 4-6.

Cindy Hinds

HOMEMADE RICOTTA CHEESE

2 quarts whole milk

3 scant teaspoons Epsom salt,
    divided

Combine milk and 2½ scant teaspoons Epsom salt in a large heavy sauce pan. Place over medium heat. Sprinkle remaining ½ teaspoon Epsom salt over top of milk—*do not stir.* Allow milk to heat and cheese will curdle to top. Using a slotted spoon, remove cheese to a bowl. Cheese will be soft, but it firms up after sitting. Use in lasagna, manicotti or omelets. May be frozen. Store in air tight container if not used immediately.

Lena Weldon

ITALIAN CHEESE MIXTURE
(for Lasagna or Manicotti)

1 recipe Homemade Ricotta
    Cheese (above)
1 egg, slightly beaten

¼ cup Parmesan cheese, grated
2 tablespoons parsley, snipped
1 clove garlic, finely chopped

Combine all ingredients and mix well. *Do not* add any salt. Cover and allow to sit in refrigerator over night before using.

Lena Weldon

MACARONI AND CHEESE

1 (8 ounce) package macaroni,
cooked
2 tablespoons butter, cut in
pieces
1¼ cups sharp cheese, cubed
(may use processed cheese
food)

½ teaspoon salt
¼ teaspoon pepper
2 eggs, beaten
3 cups milk

Combine macaroni, butter, cheese, salt and pepper. Pour into a greased two-quart baking dish. Combine eggs and milk and pour over macaroni. Sprinkle with paprika or buttered bread crumbs. Bake in a 350 degree oven for 45 minutes.

Note: May add one teaspoon onion and/or pepper flakes with the other seasonings.

June Ward

MACARONI AND CHEESE CASSEROLE

4 cups macaroni, cooked and
drained
⅓ cup butter or margarine
⅓ cup flour

2 teaspoons salt
5 cups milk
4 cups Cheddar cheese, grated
and divided

Melt butter in a heavy saucepan or double boiler. Add flour and salt, blending well. Add milk and cook, stirring constantly, until thick and smooth. Add three cups of the cheese and stir until melted and blended. Combine the macaroni noodles with the cheese sauce, mixing well. Turn mixture into a buttered casserole dish and spread remaining cup of cheese over the top. Bake twenty minutes in a 400 degree oven.

Shirley F. Burd

WELSH RAREBIT

8 ounces Cheddar cheese,
  grated
1 teaspoon dry mustard
¼ teaspoon pepper
½ teaspoon paprika

½ teaspoon Worcestershire
  sauce
4 tablespoons beer or milk
4 tablespoons butter
6 slices bread, toasted

Put grated cheese, mustard, pepper, paprika, and Worcestershire sauce in top of double boiler. Heat beer, or milk, and butter and add to cheese mixture. Heat and stir until mixture is smooth. Spread on toast and broil until brown.

Shirley F. Burd

Vegetables

ASPARAGUS CASSEROLE I

2 tablespoons butter or
  margarine
2 tablespoons flour
1/8 teaspoon nutmeg
salt and pepper to taste
1 1/2 cups milk
1 1/2 pounds fresh asparagus,
  cooked and drained

6-8 slices (thin) Swiss cheese
4 hard boiled eggs, sliced
2 cups Parmesan cheese,
  grated
2 tablespoons butter, melted
1/2 cup dry bread crumbs

Melt butter in top of a double boiler. Stir in flour, nutmeg, salt and pepper. Remove from heat; stir in milk gradually. Cook until smooth, stirring constantly. Arrange half of the asparagus in a lightly buttered casserole dish. Spoon in half of the white sauce. Add half of the Swiss cheese, a layer of egg slices and half of the Parmesan cheese. Repeat layers of asparagus, Swiss cheese, egg slices and Parmesan cheese. Spoon on the remaining white sauce. Preheat oven to 350 degrees. Combine the melted butter and bread crumbs; sprinkle crumbs over the sauce. Bake for 30-35 minutes.

Shirley F. Burd

ASPARAGUS CASSEROLE II

3 (10-ounce) packages frozen
  asparagus tips
2 (10¾-ounce) cans cream of
  mushroom soup
¾ pound sharp Cheddar
  cheese, grated

½ cup butter or margarine
2 cups cracker crumbs
½ cup blanched almonds

Cook asparagus according to package directions. Drain and save liquid. Mix a little of the liquid with the soup, just enough to make it the consistency of a sauce. Combine cheese, butter and cracker crumbs until crumbly. Preheat oven to 350 degrees. Place ½ the asparagus in a baking dish or 2 quart casserole. Sprinkle with half of the cheese-crumb mixture, then half of the nuts. Cover with half the soup. Repeat the layers saving some of the cheese and nuts to sprinkle on top. Bake for 20-30 minutes.

Note: You may want to make 3 layers, depending on the size of your dish.

Margaret Jenkins

MARINATED ASPARAGUS

½ cup vinegar
½ cup sugar
2 tablespoons lemon juice

1 (15-ounce) can asparagus
    spears, drained

Make marinade by combining vinegar, sugar and lemon juice. Pour over asparagus, cover and refrigerate overnight. Drain before serving.

Margaret Jenkins

PICKLED ASPARAGUS

1 (15-ounce) can tall green
    asparagus spears
½ cup vinegar
2 tablespoons lemon juice

½ cup sugar
salt and pepper
1 (2-ounce) can or jar whole
    pimientos

Drain asparagus thoroughly. Mix vinegar, lemon juice, sugar and dashes of salt and pepper and bring to a boil. Pour over drained asparagus and chill in refrigerator for a least 24 hours. Cut pimientos into long narrow strips and lay across "bundle" of asparagus spears tucking ends under as if tied. Serve cold. Serves 4.

Note: This recipe sounds too simple to be good but has never been served without requests for the recipe.

Nancy Willis

HOOSIER BEANS

2 (16-ounce) cans French style
    green beans
1 (10¾-ounce) can cream of
    mushroom soup

1 (2¾-ounce) package slivered
    almonds
1 (3-ounce) can French fried
    onion rings

Drain green beans and pour into a mixing bowl. Add soup, almonds and ½ can of onion rings. Stir to mix well. Spoon into a greased baking dish and top with remaining onion rings. Bake for 20 minutes. Yields 6-8 servings.

Note: May be baked in microwave oven on the high setting for 5 minutes.

Cheryl Cox

BEANS AND PEAS WITH CREAM SAUCE

3 eggs, hard boiled, chopped
fine
1½ cups mayonnaise
1½ tablespoons oil
1 tablespoon Worcestershire
sauce
1 teaspoon hot pepper sauce
1 medium onion, chopped fine

salt and pepper to taste
1 (10-ounce) package frozen
lima beans
1 (10-ounce) package frozen
green beans
1 (10-ounce) package frozen
green peas

Make sauce from eggs, mayonnaise, oil, Worcestershire, pepper sauce, onion, salt and pepper and refrigerate for 24 hours. When serving, cook lima beans, green beans, and green peas and drain. Pour cold sauce over vegetables and serve.

Marsha Robilio Keller

FRENCH GREEN BEAN CASSEROLE

1 (16-ounce) package frozen
French style green beans
1 tablespoon flour
1½ teaspoons salt
⅛ teaspoon pepper

1 teaspoon sugar
½ teaspoon onion, grated
1 cup sour cream
½ cup Swiss cheese, grated
½ cup buttered bread crumbs

Cook green beans as directed on package and drain. In a separate sauce pan, mix flour, salt, pepper, sugar, onion, sour cream and grated cheese. Mix well, stirring constantly, over low heat. Arrange cooked and drained green beans in greased baking dish. Pour cheese and cream mixture over beans and top with buttered bread crumbs. Preheat oven to 350 degrees. Bake for 20 minutes or until bubbly. Serves 4-6.

Betty Jo Walker

BROCCOLI CASSEROLE I

2 (10-ounce) packages frozen
  chopped broccoli
1 (10¾-ounce) can cream of
  mushroom soup
1 cup sharp Cheddar cheese,
  grated

¼ cup onion, minced
2 eggs, well beaten
½ cup mayonnaise
salt and pepper to taste
¾ cup cracker crumbs

Cook broccoli according to package directions. Drain. Make a sauce of the soup, cheese, onion, eggs, mayonnaise, salt and pepper. Stir broccoli into sauce and pour into a buttered 9x9 inch baking dish. Sprinkle with cracker crumbs. Bake for 40 minutes, or until hot and bubbly.

Cindy Inman

BROCCOLI CASSEROLE II

2 (10-ounce) packages frozen
  broccoli
10 ounces Velveeta cheese
½ cup butter, divided into
  halves

1 "stack pack" cheese crackers,
  crushed

Cook broccoli as directed on package; drain. Melt cheese with ½ of the butter and mix with drained broccoli. Pour into a rectangular casserole dish. Melt remaining butter and mix thoroughly with cracker crumbs. Pour crumbs over top of broccoli mixture. Preheat oven to 325 degrees. Bake until cheese is bubbly and brown, about 15 minutes.

Note: This has a tendency to burn on the bottom, so watch it carefully.

Sue Connor

BROCCOLI SOUFFLÉ

1 (10-ounce) package frozen
  chopped broccoli
2 eggs, slightly beaten
2 tablespoons flour
1½ cups Swiss cheese, grated

1 cup cottage cheese with
  chives
½ teaspoon salt
⅛ teaspoon pepper

Place broccoli in a 1½ quart glass casserole, cover with glass lid. Microwave for 6 minutes on high (100% power). Drain well. Combine eggs and flour in medium mixing bowl until smooth. Stir in the broccoli, cheeses, salt and pepper. Pour into the glass casserole and cover with lid. Microwave for 22 to 24 minutes on simmer (50% power) or until almost set in center. Let stand 5 minutes before serving. Serves 4-6.

Lynne Gorline

WEST COAST BROCCOLI

2 (10-ounce) packages frozen
  broccoli
1 (8-ounce) jar Cheese spread
2 tablespoons raw onion,
  minced, or 1 tablespoon dried
  onions

1 cup cooked rice
1 (10½-ounce) can cream of
  celery soup

Cook broccoli for 5 minutes and drain; cut into small pieces. In a saucepan, melt cheese and then add onion, cooked rice and cream of celery soup. Cook and stir over low heat for 3 or 4 minutes. Preheat oven to 350 degrees. Combine cheese mixture with broccoli. Pour into greased 1½ quart casserole dish. Bake for 30 minutes. Serves 4-6.

Beverly E. Skipper

CARROT SOUFFLÉ

1½ cups carrots, cooked and
  mashed
1 tablespoon onion, grated
2 egg yolks, beaten
salt and pepper to taste

½ cup thick cream sauce
1 tablespoon butter or
  margarine
2 egg whites

To prepared carrots, add grated onion, beaten egg yolks, salt, pepper, cream sauce and butter. Stir until mixed well. Preheat oven to 350 degrees. Beat egg whites. Fold stiffly beaten egg whites into carrot mixture. Pour into greased 1½ quart baking dish or soufflé dish. Place baking dish in pan of water (have one inch water in pan). Bake for 20-25 minutes.

Variation: Omit the grated onion. Add a dash of sugar and nutmeg.

Martha Risner

COPPER CARROTS

2 pounds carrots, scraped
  and sliced medium thin
½ cup salad oil
½ cup vinegar
⅔ cup sugar
1 tablespoon mustard

1 (10¾-ounce) tomato soup,
  undiluted
1 medium-sized bell pepper,
  diced
1 medium onion, diced

Cook carrots in salted water until medium done (about 10 minutes). Drain and cool. Combine oil, vinegar, sugar, mustard, soup, pepper and onion. Toss carrots lightly into mixture. Cover and marinate at least 24 hours in refrigerator.

Note: This will keep 2-3 weeks in refrigerator.

Mary L. Morris

MARINATED CARROTS

5 cups sliced carrots, cooked
  and drained, or 2 to 3 cans
  canned carrots, drained
1 medium white onion, sliced or
  chopped
1 small green pepper, sliced or
  chopped
1 can condensed tomato soup

½ cup salad oil
¾ cup vinegar
1 teaspoon prepared mustard
1 teaspoon Worcestershire
  sauce
1 teaspoon salt
1 teaspoon pepper

Toss sliced vegetables in a large bowl. Mix soup and other ingredients in a small bowl until blended, then pour over tossed vegetables. Let marinate in refrigerator for 12 hours. Drain and serve.

Note: Marinade may be reused or used as salad dressing.

Jane Miller

MUSTARD GLAZED CARROTS

2 pounds carrots
1 teaspoon salt
¼ cup brown sugar
3 tablespoons butter

3 tablespoons prepared
  mustard
⅛ cup parsley, chopped

Scrape carrots and cut in half lengthwise, then into 2-3 inch sections. Cook covered in water with the salt until tender, about 20 minutes. Drain. Cook sugar, butter and mustard approximately 3 minutes, until syrupy. Pour over carrots and simmer 5 minutes. Sprinkle with parsley before serving. Serves 6.

Pat Hickman

SWEET AND SOUR CARROTS

10 carrots
2 tablespoons brown mustard
¼ cup brown sugar

2 tablespoons dark corn syrup
2 tablespoons butter

Pare carrots and cut into 1 inch chunks. Steam until tender (5-10 minutes). Meanwhile, put remaining ingredients into a sauce pan. Heat, stirring constantly until smooth and blended. Drain carrots and pour sauce over carrots before serving. Serves 4.

Patti Scott

FRENCH FRIED CAULIFLOWER

2 pounds cauliflower flowerets
3 cups cracker meal
4 eggs

salt and pepper to taste
4 cups homogenized milk

Cook cauliflower for 5 minutes in boiling water, then drain. Add salt and popper to cracker meal. Whip eggs and add milk to whipped egg mixture, then add cauliflower. Let soak for 5 minutes and drain. Add drained cauliflower to cracker meal mixture. Fry in hot cooking oil for 5 minutes or until brown. Serve warm.

Margaret Toler

CREAMED CELERY

4 cups celery, cut diagonally
  into ½ inch pieces
2 tablespoons butter
2 tablespoons flour

2 cups milk
1 teaspoon salt
¾ cup pecan halves
½ cup buttered bread crumbs

Cook celery in small amount of boiling water until tender. Drain well. Melt butter in a saucepan over medium heat. Stir in flour. Add milk slowly to make a cream sauce. Stir and cook until thick and smooth. Preheat oven to 400 degrees. Add salt and drained celery. Spoon into a greased 1½ quart casserole dish. Top with pecans, then sprinkle with buttered bread crumbs. Bake for 15 minutes. Serves 6.

Joyce Montgomery

SUCCOTASH

1 cup corn, cooked
1 cup lima beans, cooked
¼ cup milk

1 tablespoon butter
salt and pepper to taste

Combine corn, lima beans and milk. Bring to a boil. Season to taste. Add butter and serve. Serves 4.

Shirley F. Burd

SQUAW CORN

4 slices bacon, diced
2 tablespoons onion, chopped
½ bell pepper, chopped
3 cups corn, cooked (canned or
   fresh)

¼ cup pimiento, diced
   (optional)

Brown bacon in a skillet. Remove bacon from the skillet and sauté onion and pepper in the remaining bacon grease. Drain. Stir in corn and pimiento, if desired. Simmer 5 minutes.

Pat Worley

EGGPLANT SUPREME

1 large eggplant, peeled and
   cubed
1 bell pepper, chopped
2 ribs celery, chopped
1 large onion, chopped
¼ cup butter
1 teaspoon Worcestershire
   sauce

dash hot pepper sauce
1 cup sharp Cheddar cheese,
   grated
1 cup ripe olives, sliced
salt to taste
1 cup cracker crumbs
Parmesan cheese (optional)

Steam eggplant in small amount of water on low heat until tender. Drain. Sauté pepper, celery, and onion in butter. Add eggplant, Worcestershire sauce and hot pepper sauce and stir. Add grated cheese and olives. Salt to taste. Preheat oven to 375 degrees. Place in buttered baking dish and cover with cracker crumbs. Bake 30 minutes. Sprinkle with Parmesan cheese, if desired.

Margaret Jenkins

BRANDY FRUIT CASSEROLE

1 (16-ounce) can peach halves, drained
1 (8-ounce) can apricots, drained
1 (16-ounce) can pear halves, drained
3 (8-ounce) can pineapple chunks, drained

1 (4-ounce) jar maraschino cherries, drained
⅓ cup butter, melted
½ cup brown sugar
½ cup white sugar
½ cup brandy
2 tablespoons butter

Preheat oven to 325 degrees. Combine fruits and place in a shallow baking dish. Put butter, sugars and brandy in a saucepan and heat until sugars dissolve Pour over fruit. Dot with 2 tablespoons butter. Bake for 1 hour. Cool and refrigerate for 24 hours before serving.

Margaret Jenkins

SHERRIED FRUIT COMPOTE

1 (16-ounce) can black pitted cherries, drained
1 (16-ounce) can sliced peaches
1 (16-ounce) can pineapple chunks

1 (16-ounce) can pear halves
1 (16-ounce) can fruit for salads
½ cup cream sherry
¼ cup lemon juice
1 tablespoon cornstarch

Preheat oven to 350 degrees. Drain fruits and reserve liquids. Combine fruits and place in a large casserole dish. Combine sherry, lemon juice and ¾ cup of the reserved fruit juices. Pour over the fruit. Bake for 20 minutes. Sprinkle with cornstarch and shake gently to mix in. Bake 10 more minutes. Serve with a main dish as you would a vegetable.

Note: Adjust the amounts of sherry, lemon juice and fresh fruit juices according to your own tastes, keeping the total of liquids to 1½ cups.

Brenda Y. Smith

JIM BOWN'S NOODLES

⅞ cup flour
1 egg

⅓ teaspoon oil
⅓ teaspoon salt

Mound flour on pastry board. Put egg, oil and salt into a depression in the flour and mix with a wooden spoon. Put ball of pastry into a wet paper towel to a thickness of ¹⁄₁₆ to ⅛ inch. Cut into preferred shape and sizes. Dry for 30-60 minutes. Boil until tender in water with a pinch of salt.

Note: These are great for beef stroganoff. If using as a vegetable, toss with 2 tablespoons butter or margarine, and possibly, grated Romano or Parmesan cheese.

Shirley F. Burd

ONION CHEESE CASSEROLE

4 large onions
½ cup flour
2½ cups milk

1 teaspoon salt
3 eggs
¼ pound Swiss cheese, grated

Preheat oven to 350 degrees. Peel and slice onions. Combine flour, milk, salt and eggs. Beat well. Grease a large shallow baking dish and place in it half of the onion slices in a single layer. Sprinkle with half of the cheese. Cover with remaining onion slices, then sprinkle with remaining cheese. Pour milk mixture over layers. Bake for 35-40 minutes. Serves 8.

Pat Worley

POTATO CASSEROLE I

4-5 medium size potatoes
1 cup sour cream
2 cups cottage cheese

1 tablespoon onion, grated
salt and pepper to taste

Cook and slice potatoes. Preheat oven to 350 degrees. Mix sour cream, cheese, onion, salt and pepper. Combine with potatoes and pour into a 1 quart casserole. Bake for 30 minutes.

Pat Worley

ENGLISH PEA CASSEROLE

2 (17-ounce) cans English peas, (small new peas), drained
1 (8-ounce) can sliced water chestnuts, with liquid
1 (4-ounce) jar chopped pimiento
¼ cup butter or margarine
1 medium-size onion, diced
1 cup celery, diced
2 tablespoons bell pepper, chopped
1 (10¾-ounce) can mushroom soup, undiluted
½ cup cracker crumbs
2 tablespoons butter

Combine peas and chestnuts with liquid and pimiento. Melt butter and sauté onion, celery and pepper until soft. Mix with peas and chestnuts. Preheat oven to 350 degrees. Place half of the vegetable mixture in a buttered 2 quart casserole. Cover with half of the soup. Add remainder of vegetables, then, remainder of soup. Sprinkle with cracker crumbs and dot with butter. Bake for 45 minutes or until bubbly and thick.

Mary L. Morris

CREAMED POTATOES

1 cup potatoes, cooked and diced
2 tablespoons butter
2 tablespoons flour
⅛ teaspoon salt
⅛ teaspoon paprika, hot Hungarian type
1 cup milk
1 tablespoon chives, chopped (optional)

Prepare potatoes. In a double boiler, melt the butter, adding flour, salt and paprika. Mix until smooth. Add the milk gradually and continue to mix until smooth. Cook until thickened, stirring occasionally. Add the potatoes and chives. Serve when hot.

Note: A whisk surpasses the use of a spoon in making this cream sauce. This recipe may be increased without problem. It's a good use for left-over potatoes.

Shirley F. Burd

POTATO CASSEROLE II

6 medium size white potatoes
2 cups Cheddar cheese,
  shredded
16 ounces sour cream

⅓ cup onion, chopped
salt and pepper to taste
6 tablespoons butter (divided
  into 2 portions)

Boil, chill, peel and shred potatoes. Fold in cheese, sour cream, onion, salt and pepper. Preheat oven to 350 degrees. Spray a large casserole dish with a vegetable cooking spray. Then, dot it with half of the butter. Pour potato mixture into the dish and dot with remaining butter. Bake for 30 minutes.

Peggy Sparrenberger

SOUR CREAM POTATOES

6 medium potatoes
1½ cups mayonnaise
1 cup sour cream
1½ teaspoons prepared
  horseradish (optional)
½ teaspoon salt

2 medium size onions chopped
  fine, or equivalent in
  dehydrated flakes
1 teaspoon celery seed
1 tablespoon parsley or chives,
  chopped

Cook potatoes, cool and slice thin. Combine mayonnaise, sour cream, horseradish, salt, onion, and celery seed. In a deep casserole, layer ⅓ of potatoes, then ⅓ of sour cream mixture. Repeat layers, ending with sour cream mixture. Sprinkle with parsley or chives. Store covered in refrigerator overnight or at least, 6 hours before serving.

The Committee

CREAMED SPINACH

1 (10-ounce) package frozen
  spinach
1 (10¾-ounce) can cream of
  mushroom soup

juice of 1 medium lemon

Place all ingredients in a medium saucepan and cook over low heat until spinach thaws (about 20-25 minutes).

Note: Do not add any water to either spinach or soup!

Karen Patterson

QUICK SKILLET POTATOES
(15 minutes)

1 (16-ounce) can whole, cooked potatoes
2 tablespoons butter
3 tablespoons green onions, chopped
1 teaspoon parsley, chopped

2 (1-ounce) slices American cheese, grated
2 tablespoons Parmesan cheese
salt and pepper to taste

Drain potatoes and dry with paper towel. Slice into ¼ inch rounds. Heat butter in skillet; add potatoes and onion. Cook until potatoes are slightly browned. Add parsley, salt and pepper. Add cheese and cook until cheese melts. Do not stir excessively. Serve at once. Serves 2.

Martha C. Yancey

RATATOUILLE

1½ to 2 pounds eggplant, peeled and cubed
1½ to 2 pounds zucchini, sliced ½ inch thick
2 cups green pepper, sliced into 1 inch squares
3 pounds tomatoes, peeled, seeded and cut into strips
2½ cups onion, thinly sliced or chopped

2 teaspoons garlic, finely chopped
¼ to ½ cup olive oil
½ cup fresh parsley, chopped
2 tablespoons fresh basil, chopped (or 2 teaspoons dried basil)
1 tablespoon salt
1 teaspoon black pepper

Prepare all vegetables as listed above. Place cubed eggplant in cold water and soak until ready to use. Sauté onion and garlic in oil until crisp tender. Drain eggplant thoroughly and add to onion and garlic. Cook for 10 minutes. Add zucchini and pepper, stirring the vegetables well to mix. Then, add parsley, basil, salt and pepper. Cook and stir for 10 minutes. Add tomatoes and cook the Ratatouille down to the consistency you prefer. The vegetables taste best if they are still slightly crisp and chunky. Serve hot or cold.

Linda White

SPECIAL SPINACH

2 (10-ounce) packages frozen
   chopped spinach, cooked
   and drained well
1½ cups sour cream
¾ cup Parmesan cheese

salt and pepper to taste
1 teaspoon garlic powder
¼ cup butter
bread crumbs

Preheat oven to 350 degrees. Mix all ingredients together except the bread crumbs and put in a greased 8x11 inch Pyrex dish. Cover generously with bread crumbs. Bake for 20-25 minutes.

Mary Pat Van Epps

SPINACH CASSEROLE

1 (16-ounce) package frozen
   chopped spinach
3 eggs, beaten
3 tablespoons flour

1 pint cottage cheese
¼ pound sharp Cheddar
   cheese, cubed
2 tablespoons butter

Preheat oven to 350 degrees. Thaw spinach and mix with eggs, flour, cottage cheese and Cheddar cheese. Pour into a greased 1 quart baking dish. Dot with butter and bake uncovered for 45 minutes. Yields 4-6 servings.

Brenda Thoresen

SPINACH BALLS (OR SPINACH CASSEROLE)

2 (10-ounce) packages frozen
   chopped spinach
2 cups herb stuffing
1 cup Parmesan cheese, grated

4 eggs, beaten
½ cup butter or margarine,
   softened

Preheat oven to 350 degrees. Cook spinach and drain dry. Combine with all ingredients and roll into bite-size balls. Place on cookie sheets. Bake for 10-12 minutes. If casserole is desired, mix spinach with stuffing, eggs and butter. Place in a greased 2 quart baking dish. Sprinkle with Parmesan cheese and bake for 30 minutes.

Note: The unbaked Spinach Balls may be frozen for later use.

Libby Parks

EXCELLENT SPINACH

3 (10-ounce) packages frozen
   chopped spinach
1 tablespoon lemon juice
16 ounces sour cream
½ cup Parmesan cheese

1 teaspoon seasoning salt
1 teaspoon garlic salt
salt and pepper to taste
½ cup crushed crackers
3 tablespoons margarine

Preheat oven to 350 degrees. Cook spinach according to package directions. Cool and drain. Add lemon juice, sour cream, cheese, seasoning salt, salt and pepper. Brown crushed crackers in margarine. Pour spinach mixture into a buttered casserole and top with browned cracker crumbs. Bake for 30-40 minutes.

Note: The casserole dish may be sprayed with a vegetable shortening spray rather than being buttered.

Peggy Sparrenberger

LEAH'S FAMOUS SQUASH CASSEROLE

3 cups squash, thinly sliced
1 cup onion, chopped
1 cup celery, chopped
1 cup green pepper, chopped
3 tablespoons butter or
  margarine
1 tablespoon flour
2 tablespoons margarine
salt and pepper to taste
1½ cups American cheese,
  grated
2 cups buttered bread crumbs

Cook squash in very little water until tender (about 5-7 minutes). Sauté onion, celery and green pepper in 3 tablespoons of butter and add to the cooked squash. Make a roux using the flour and margarine. Add the roux to vegetables and cook for about three minutes. Season with salt and pepper. Preheat oven to 350 degrees. Pour ½ of the vegetable mixture into a buttered 2 quart casserole. Sprinkle with half of the grated cheese and half of the crumbs. Repeat layers with remaining vegetable mixture, cheese and crumbs. Bake about 30 minutes or until crumbs are golden brown.

Dorothy Griscom

SQUASH CASSEROLE II

1 pound summer squash,
  sliced, or 2 (10-ounce)
  packages frozen squash
⅓ cup (5 crackers) saltines,
  crumbled
1 onion, finely chopped
2 tablespoons margarine,
  melted (or bacon drippings)
½ cup celery, finely diced
2 tablespoons green pepper,
  diced
½ cup Cheddar cheese, grated
2 eggs, beaten
1 (5.33-ounce) can evaporated
  milk
¼ teaspoon salt
pepper to taste

Cook and drain squash. Combine squash with remaining ingredients. Preheat oven to 375 degrees. Place in a buttered 2 quart casserole. Bake for 25 minutes. Serves 6.

Dorothy Griscom

SQUASH CASSEROLE III

2 cups squash, sliced
1 onion, chopped
¼ cup butter
¼ cup flour
2 cups milk

2 eggs, beaten
4 ounces Cheddar cheese,
    grated
salt and pepper to taste
¼ cup buttered bread crumbs

Preheat oven to 350 degrees. Cook squash and onion together until soft. Melt butter, add flour and mix. Add milk and cook for 5 minutes, stirring frequently. Add eggs, cheese, salt and pepper, mixing well to blend all ingredients. Combine with vegetables. Pour into a greased 1½ quart casserole. Top with buttered bread crumbs. Bake for 40-60 minutes.

Jean Wall

SWEET POTATO CASSEROLE I

3-4 pounds sweet potatoes
½ teaspoon salt
1 teaspoon vanilla
¼ cup butter, melted
1 cup granulated sugar
½ cup whipping cream (or light
    cream)

2 eggs, beaten
3 tablespoons butter
1 cup brown sugar
⅓ cup flour
1 cup coconut
1 cup pecans, chopped

Boil, peel and mash sweet potatoes. Add salt, vanilla, melted butter, granulated sugar, cream and eggs. Cream this mixture with mixer and pour into a greased 2 quart casserole. Preheat oven to 325 degrees. Make topping by mixing the remaining butter, brown sugar, flour, coconut and pecans. Sprinkle over potatoes. Bake uncovered for 25-30 minutes. If topping browns too fast, cover with foil. Serves 8.

Linda White

SWEET POTATO CASSEROLE II

2 cups sweet potatoes, mashed
(2 large potatoes cooked in
   jackets)
2 eggs, beaten
6 tablespoons butter or
   margarine
1 (13-ounce) can evaporated
   milk
1¼ cups granulated sugar

⅛ teaspoon mace
1 teaspoon vanilla
1½ ounce bourbon
6 tablespoons butter or
   margarine
¼ cup coconut
½ cup brown sugar
½ cup nuts, chopped
1 cup cornflakes, crushed

Preheat oven to 350 degrees. Mix well potatoes, eggs, butter, milk, granulated sugar, mace, vanilla and bourbon. Pour into a baking dish. Bake for 30 minutes. Combine butter with coconut, brown sugar, nuts and cornflakes until crumbly. Sprinkle over cooked casserole. Return to oven and brown.

Rosemarie Ward

RACHEL'S SWEET POTATO PUDDING

¼ cup butter
1 cup milk
½ cup granulated sugar
½ cup brown sugar
3 eggs, beaten
pinch of salt
1 teaspoon vanilla

½ teaspoon nutmeg
½ teaspoon cinnamon
1 (29-ounce) can sweet
   potatoes or yams, drained
   (reserve ¼ cup liquid)
2 tablespoons butter
1 cup marshmallows

Preheat oven to 350 degrees. Heat together butter, milk and sugars. Remove from heat and add eggs, salt, vanilla, nutmeg and cinnamon. Mix well. Add drained potatoes and the reserved liquid. Blend in electric blender for several seconds. Pour into a 2 quart casserole and bake for 30 minutes. Dot top with butter, and add marshmallows and return to oven to brown.

Armantine Keller

SCALLOPED TOMATOES

1 (28 ounce) can whole
tomatoes and juice
1½ cups croutons or
4 slices bread spread with
garlic butter, toasted and
cubed
½ onion, minced

¼ cup butter or margarine,
melted
1 cup Mozzarella cheese, cubed
1 cup Cheddar cheese, cubed
½ teaspoon salt
¼ teaspoon pepper

Preheat oven to 375 degrees. Combine all ingredients and place in greased 1½ to 2 quart casserole. Bake for 20 minutes.

Mary Pat Van Epps

TOMATO PUDDING

½ cup butter or margarine
2 cups bread cubes
1 (10½-ounce) tomato puree

¼ cup water
¼ teaspoon salt
1 cup light brown sugar

Melt butter, pour over bread cubes and toss. Heat tomato puree with water, salt and brown sugar. Simmer for 5 minutes. Preheat oven to 325 degrees. Pour mixture over bread cubes, toss and pour into 1½ quart casserole. Bake covered for 45 minutes. Use as a side dish with meat or other vegetable. Serves 8.

Dorothy Griscom

SOUL FOOD: CANDIED YAMS

4 large sweet potatoes
1 cup brown sugar
⅓ cup water

3 tablespoons butter
¼ teaspoon nutmeg

Wash sweet potatoes and boil in their jackets until tender. Preheat oven to 350 degrees. Slice potatoes lengthwise and arrange in baking dish. Mix sugar and water and bring to a boil. Pour over potatoes, dot with butter and sprinkle with nutmeg. Bake for 30 minutes, basting several times.

Myra S. Tillis

MARINATED VEGETABLES

2 bunches fresh broccoli
2 heads fresh cauliflower
1 cup cider vinegar
1 tablespoon sugar
1 tablespoon dill seed

1 tablespoon salt
1 teaspoon pepper, coarsely
  ground
1 clove garlic, minced
1½ cups vegetable oil

Cut the broccoli and cauliflower into small flowerets, wash well, and place in a glass bowl or pan. Make marinade by thoroughly mixing vinegar, sugar, dill, salt, pepper, garlic and oil. Pour marinade over vegetables, cover and refrigerate for 24 hours. Baste vegetables with the marinade occasionally. Drain and serve chilled.

Note: The broccoli may be arranged on a platter in the shape of a Christmas tree, using one of the large stems as the trunk. Place cherry tomatoes on the tree for Christmas balls. Arrange marinated cauliflower around the tree as background.

Dorothy Griscom

ZUCCHINI WITH BEANS

2 medium zucchini, sliced
¼ cup salad oil (or bacon
  drippings)
1 (16-ounce) can green beans,
  drained (reserve liquid)

½ cup onion, sliced
1 clove garlic, minced
1 tablespoon soy sauce
toasted almonds

Sauté zucchini in oil (or bacon drippings). Drain. Add beans, onion, garlic and soy sauce. If necessary, add a small amount of reserved bean liquid to keep ingredients from being too dry. Mix and heat thoroughly. Garnish with almonds and serve at once.

Bonnie Brown

Breads and Rolls

ANGEL BISCUITS

1 package active dry yeast
2 tablespoons water, warm
5 cups flour
1 teaspoon soda
1 teaspoon baking powder

2 tablespoons sugar
1½ teaspoons salt
1 cup vegetable shortening
2 cups buttermilk
½ cup butter, melted

Preheat oven to 400 degrees. Dissolve yeast in water, according to directions on the package. Sift flour, soda, baking powder, sugar and salt into large bowl. Cut in shortening until finely crumbed. Add buttermilk and yeast mixture; mix well. Turn onto a floured board and knead 1-2 minutes. Roll to ½ inch thickness; cut with biscuit cutter. Place on baking sheet; brush tops with melted butter. Bake for 12 to 15 minutes.

Note: Dough may be refrigerated in covered bowl for several days. Remove portion of dough needed for meal 1 hour before baking.

Margaret Jenkins

DROP BISCUITS

1½ cups self-rising flour
1 egg, powdered or fresh
2 tablespoons powdered milk

4 tablespoons vegetable oil
½ cup water

Preheat oven to 350 degrees. Mix dry ingredients together. Then, add oil and water and stir until blended. Drop by teaspoon onto greased pan. Bake approximately 10 minutes. May need to be browned under broiler.

Mary Mayhue

MAYONNAISE BISCUITS

2 cups self-rising flour, sifted   **¼ cup mayonnaise**
2 tablespoons sugar (optional)   **1 cup milk**

Preheat oven to 375 degrees. Sift flour, measure and place in mixing bowl. Blend in sugar, mayonnaise and milk. Pour into greased, hot muffin cups. Fill cups ⅔ full. Bake for 12 to 15 minutes until brown.

Note: Do not substitute salad dressing for mayonnaise.

Joan Dodson

APPLE NUT BREAD OR CAKE

1½ cups oil   **1 teaspoon cinnamon**
2 cups sugar   **½ teaspoon nutmeg**
2 eggs   **1 teaspoon vanilla**
2½ cups flour   **1 cup pecans, chopped**
1 teaspoon salt   **3 cups apples, peeled and**
1 teaspoon soda   **chopped (about 4 medium)**
2 teaspoons baking powder

Preheat oven to 350 degrees. Mix oil, sugar and eggs. Sift dry ingredients together, including cinnamon and nutmeg, and add to egg and sugar mixture. Beat well and add vanilla, nuts and apples. Pour batter into 2 greased and floured loaf pans or a tube pan. Bake for 1 hour.

ICING FOR APPLE NUT CAKE (use if served as a cake)
½ cup butter or margarine   **1 teaspoon vanilla**
1 cup brown sugar
¼ cup cream (may use canned
   evaporated milk)

Heat butter and sugar until melted. Add cream and let come to a full boil. Boil for 1-2 minutes. Let cool and add vanilla. Pour over warm cake.

Tine Keller

BEER BREAD I

3 cups self-rising flour   **1 (12 ounce) can beer**
3 tablespoons sugar

Preheat oven to 350 degrees. Mix ingredients thoroughly and pour into greased 9x5 inch loaf pan. Bake for 1 hour or until well browned.

Note: For a different texture, add ¼ cup wheat bran and ¼ cup liquid oil. If plain flour is used, add 1 tablespoon baking powder and ½ teaspoon salt per cup flour.

Joan Dodson

BEER BREAD II

3 cups self-rising flour, unsifted   **4 ounces butter, melted**
3 tablespoons sugar
10 ounces beer, room
  temperature

Preheat oven to 350 degrees. Mix flour, sugar and beer together. Dough will be very sticky. Pour dough into greased 9x5 inch loaf pan. Pour melted butter over dough. Bake for 1 hour. Serves 4-6 people.

Kay Fallin

BANANA BREAD

2 cups sifted flour   **½ cup milk**
1 cup sugar   **1 cup bananas, mashed**
2½ teaspoons baking powder   **1 egg, well beaten**
¾ teaspoon salt   **2 tablespoons shortening,**
¾ cup Grape Nut Cereal   **melted**

Preheat oven to 350 degrees. Sift flour, sugar, baking powder and salt into bowl. Stir in dry cereal. In a mixing bowl, blend milk, bananas, egg and shortening. Add flour mixture, stirring just until all flour is moistened. Pour batter into a 9x5 inch loaf pan. Bake for 1 hour or until cake tester comes out clean. Cool in pan for 10 minutes; then, turn out onto cake rack to finish cooling.

Pat Meade

HOT WATER CORN BREAD

2 cups corn meal
1 teaspoon flour
1 teaspoon sugar

1 teaspoon salt
4 cups water, boiling

Mix dry ingredients. Pour into boiling water and stir until well mixed. Drop by spoon into hot shortening in a skillet. Fry until brown. Makes about 12 cakes.

Janie Lewis

CRANBERRY BREAD

2 cups flour
1 cup sugar
2 teaspoons baking powder
½ teaspoon salt
½ teaspoon soda
1 egg, beaten

¾ cup orange juice
¼ cup orange rind, finely grated
2 tablespoons vegetable oil
½ cup pecans, chopped
2 cups cranberries, cut in
   halves

Preheat oven to 325 degrees. Sift dry ingredients into mixing bowl. Add egg, juice, rind, and oil. Mix until dampened. Add nuts and cranberries; mix again. Bake in greased loaf pan for 50 minutes. Makes 1 loaf.

Patty Scott

CORN LIGHT BREAD

2 quarts (8 cups) water, divided
3 quarts (12 cups) corn meal,
  sifted and divided
1 tablespoon salt
1 cup sugar
2 tablespoons lard, melted

3 eggs, beaten
1½ cups buttermilk
1 tablespoon soda (dissolved in
  buttermilk)
2¼ cups flour

In a 6 to 7 quart pot, boil 1 quart (4 cups) water. Sift in 1 quart corn meal stirring constantly. Remove from heat and let cool. Then, stir in 1 quart lukewarm water, salt and 1 quart (4 cups) corn meal. Let mixture stand overnight in a warm place. In the morning, stir in 1 quart of corn meal, sugar, melted lard, eggs, the buttermilk in which you have dissolved the soda, and flour. Pour batter into 2 greased 9x5 inch loaf pans. Let rise in a warm place. Preheat oven to 350 degrees. Bake for 1 hour or until cake tester comes out clean. Cool in pans. Makes 2 large loaves.

Margaret Jenkins

LOAF BREAD

6 cups flour, sifted
1 teaspoon salt
½ cup sugar
4 eggs, beaten

½ cup vegetable shortening
1 package active dry yeast
2 cups water, warm

Combine flour, salt and sugar. Make a hole in the center of the flour mixture and pour in eggs and shortening. Dissolve yeast in warm water, and then, add a little at a time to flour mixture until all ingredients are mixed well. Knead dough on a floured pastry board or cloth for 5 minutes. Place dough in a greased bowl and put in the refrigerator to rise overnight. Divide dough in half and shape into two bread pans and let rise 2 hours. Preheat oven to 400 degrees. Bake for 10 minutes. Lower oven temperature to 375 degrees and bake for 30 minutes. Brush butter on top of loaf while hot. Cool loaves for 10 minutes before removing from pans. Makes 2 loaves.

Mrs. Leroy Pope

OHIO HEALTH BREAD

1 cup whole wheat flour
½ cup wheat germ
½ cup bran flakes
2 tablespoons baking soda

1 cup walnuts, chopped
2 eggs
¾ cup apple sauce
½ cup molasses

Preheat oven to 350 degrees. Mix ingredients thoroughly. Pour into a greased 9x5 inch loaf pan. Bake for 50 minutes.

Note: For smoother texture, add ¼ cup liquid shortening and ½ cup milk.

Joan Dodson

POPPY SEED BREAD

3 cups flour
1½ teaspoons salt
1½ teaspoons baking powder
2½ cups sugar
1½ cups milk

1⅛ cups salad oil
1½ tablespoons poppy seeds
3 eggs
1½ teaspoons vanilla
1½ teaspoons almond flavoring

Preheat oven to 350 degrees. Mix all ingredients in mixing bowl by hand; then beat for two minutes with electric mixer. Pour mixture into greased loaf pans. Bake for 1 hour. Glaze while still hot. Makes two 9x5 inch loaves.

POPPY SEED BREAD GLAZE
¾ cup powdered sugar
¼ cup lemon juice
2 tablespoons butter

½ teaspoon vanilla
½ teaspoon almond flavoring

Heat all ingredients in saucepan until blended; spoon gently over hot loaves and let cool before slicing to serve.

Dianna Thompson

AN EASY BATTER BLACK RYE BREAD

2¾ cups bread flour (no
   substitution)
1 cup rye flour
1 package active dry yeast
1¼ cups warm water

2 tablespoons margarine
2 tablespoons molasses
2 teaspoons salt
1¼ tablespoons caraway seed

Thoroughly combine bread and rye flours and reserve. Dissolve yeast in warm water (105 - 115 degrees) in large mixing bowl. Add margarine, molasses, salt and caraway seed. Mix well with hand or stationary beaters. Add 2 cups of the flour mixture. Beat at medium speed for 3-4 minutes. Stir in the remaining flour for a stiff batter. Cover with a towel. Let rise until doubled for 45-75 minutes, depending upon room temperature. Stir down, spread in a greased loaf pan. Cover and let rise until doubled, about an hour. Preheat oven to 375 degrees. Bake for 45-50 minutes. Remove from pan and cool on a rack (wire). Makes 1 loaf.

Note: After cooling, this rye bread may be sliced and frozen in foil, un-thawing slices as needed.

Shirley F. Burd

WHOLE WHEAT HEALTH BREAD

1½ cups whole wheat flour
1 scant tablespoon salt
2 packages active dry yeast
1 cup skim milk
1 cup water
¼ cup oil
¼ cup honey

1 egg
½ cup white flour
½ cup rye flour
½ cup whole wheat flour
2 to 4 tablespoons soy flour
¼ cup wheat germ
1 tablespoon sesame seeds

Put wheat flour, salt and yeast into mixing bowl. Heat milk, water, oil, and honey to 110 degrees. Add to flour in bowl and stir to blend. Add egg and beat 3 minutes on medium speed with electric mixer. Mix the remaining flours, and wheat germ; add to mixture in bowl and stir to make a sticky dough. Cover and let rise in a warm place for about 1 hour. Preheat oven to 375 degrees. Stir dough down and turn into greased 9x5 inch loaf pan. Sprinkle sesame seeds on top of dough. Bake for 30-35 minutes.

Claire Borkert

HONEY WHOLE WHEAT BREAD

1 cup milk	2½ cups whole wheat flour
1 cup water	2 (½ ounce) packages active
½ cup honey	dry yeast
3 tablespoons butter	1 large egg
3½ to 4 cups all purpose flour	1 tablespoon salt

Heat milk, water, honey and butter to 120 degrees. In a large bowl combine 2 cups all purpose flour, 1 cup whole wheat flour, yeast, egg, and salt. Pour warm milk mixture over dry ingredients. Mix for 3 minutes (use electric mixer with dough hooks if you have them). Gradually, add remaining flour to form a stiff dough. Mix until smooth and satiny, about 4 minutes. Place dough in a greased bowl. Turn once to grease top of dough. Cover and let rise about 1 hour, or until the dough is doubled in size. Punch down dough and knead on a floured surface until the dough is elastic. Divide dough in half and shape into loaves. Put loaves into greased 9x5 inch loaf pans; cover and let rise 1½ hours or until dough is doubled in size. Preheat oven to 375 degrees. Bake for 10 minutes, then reduce heat to 350 degrees and bake 30 to 35 minutes longer. Remove from pans and cool on wire rack. To keep from drying, slice as needed. Makes 2 loaves.

Note: If you do not have loaf pans, the dough can be shaped into 2 large rounds and baked on crock or iron stone plates. Then, the loaves look much more original.

Martha C. Yancey

BRAN MUFFINS

1 cup bran cereal	1 cup sifted flour
¾ cup milk	2½ teaspoons baking powder
1 egg, beaten	½ teaspoon salt
¼ cup shortening, softened	¼ cup sugar

Combine bran cereal and milk in mixing bowl. Let stand until most of milk is absorbed by the cereal. Add egg and shortening; beat well. Sift together flour, baking powder, salt and sugar. Add to cereal mixture stirring until flour is moist (do not beat). Fill greased muffin cups ⅔ full. Bake at 400 degrees for 25 minutes. Makes 12 muffins.

Pat Meade

WHITE BREAD

5 to 6 cups Bread Flour (no substitution)
3½ tablespoons sugar
2 teaspoons salt
2 (¼ ounce) packages active dry yeast

2 cups water
¼ cup oil
1 egg

Grease 2 loaf pans and 1 large bowl. In another large bowl, combine 2 cups flour, sugar, salt and yeast. Blend well. Heat water and oil to 120 to 125 degrees using a candy thermometer. Add to the dry mixture. Blend until moistened at low speed, then beat for 2 to 3 minutes at medium-high speed. Stir in the remainder of the flour until the dough pulls away from the bowl. Turn dough onto a floured pastry cloth and knead thoroughly. (The kneading takes 10 to 12 minutes or until dough is smooth and elastic and has blisters under the surface which break as you knead). Put dough in the greased bowl, turning once to grease the top of the dough. Cover with a towel and let rise until the dough doubles in size. Depending on the room temperature this will be 1½ to 2½ hours. Punch down dough to release air. Divide dough into two parts, cover with a towel and let rest for 15 minutes. Remove all air bubbles by rolling with a rolling pin to a 9x13 inch rectangle on a lightly floured pastry cloth. Roll dough up tucking under the ends and place seam side down in a loaf pan. Repeat with the other half of the dough. Cover pans and let dough rise until it is ½ to 1 inch above the edge of the pans (about 1 to 2 hours). Preheat oven to 375 degrees. Brush top of bread with a beaten egg and bake for 45 to 55 minutes. Remove from pan and cool on wire racks. Brush tops with butter.

Note: When cool, this bread can be sliced and wrapped for freezing.

Shirley F. Burd

BEER MUFFINS

3 cups prepared buscuit mix
3 tablespoons sugar

1 cup beer

Preheat oven to 375 degrees. Mix ingredients and drop into greased muffin cups. Bake for 20 minutes. Makes 12 muffins.

Judy Pinson

ZUCCHINI BREAD

3 eggs beaten
2 cups sugar
1 tablespoon vanilla
1 cup oil
2 cups zucchini, peeled, cored
   and grated

3 cups flour
1 teaspoon salt
1 teaspoon soda
1 tablespoon cinnamon
¼ teaspoon baking powder
1 cup nuts, chopped

Preheat oven to 350 degrees. Cream eggs, sugar, vanilla, oil, and zucchini. Sift flour, salt, soda, cinnamon and baking powder. Add to creamed mixture and mix well. Stir in nuts and pour into 2 greased and floured loaf pans. Bake for 1 hour. Remove from pans immediately.

Margaret Jenkins

BRIOCHE

½ cup milk, scalded
½ cup margarine
⅓ cup sugar
1 teaspoon salt
1 package active dry yeast
¼ cup water, warm

3 eggs
1 egg yolk
3½ cups *bread* flour (no
   substitution)
1 egg white
1 tablespoon sugar

Cook scalded milk to lukewarm. Cream margarine, sugar and salt in a large bowl. Add yeast to 105 to 115 degee warm water and stir until dissolved. To the creamed mixture, add lukewarm milk, dissolved yeast, eggs, egg yolk, and flour, in order. With a wooden spoon, beat well for 2 minutes. Cover with a towel and let rise until double in size. Stir down and beat well with spoon for 2 minutes. Cover with foil and refrigerate overnight. Beat down and turn dough onto a floured pastry cloth. With ¼ of the dough, make 24 tiny balls. With the remainder of the dough, make 24 large balls. Grease muffin cups; place a large ball in each cup. Make a *deep* indentation in each of the large balls with your finger that is damp-ened slightly with cold water. Insert a small ball into each indentation. Cover and let rise until doubled in size. Preheat oven to 350 degrees. Brush each roll with egg white and sugar mixture. Bake for 15 to 20 minutes.

Shirley F. Burd

CINNAMON YEAST ROLLS

3½ cups flour
1 package dry yeast
1¼ cups milk
¼ cup sugar

¼ cup butter
1 teaspoon salt
1 egg

Roll Filling:
1 cup sugar
1½ teaspoons cinnamon

½ cup butter, melted
raisins

In a large mixing bowl, combine flour and the yeast. Heat milk, sugar, butter and salt just until warm (115-120 degrees), stirring until butter melts. Add to dry mixture. Add egg. Beat at low speed until mixed, then beat 3 minutes at high speed. By hand, stir in remaining flour to make a soft dough. Shape into a ball. Place in a lightly greased container turning once to grease all surfaces. Cover and refrigerate for a least 2 hours. (Can be refrigerated over night so you can save time the day you plan on serving the rolls). About 2 hours before serving, remove dough from refrigerator and roll ½ of dough out a a time on lightly floured surface into a 8x16 inch rectangle. Mix the sugar and cinnamon together with butter. Brush on dough. Sprinkle with raisins. Roll up into long roll, sealing the edges. Cut in 1 inch slices using a thread crisscrossed at top. Place in greased 11x16 inch pan. Cover and let rise about 1 hour or until doubled in size. Preheat oven to 350 degrees. Bake for 20 minutes. Frost while still hot. Makes about 30 rolls.

Note: This recipe can also be used for rolls. Omit sweet roll filling and icing. Roll dough to ½ inch thickness and cut out or shape. Cover and let rise until doubled in bulk. Preheat oven to 400 degrees. Bake on greased sheet for 10 to 12 minutes. Yield: 2 to 3 dozen rolls.

Frosting for Cinnamon Rolls
1 (16 ounce) box powdered
   sugar

6 tablespoons milk

Mix sugar and milk together and spread on hot rolls. Ices about 30 rolls. Can be doubled.

Mary Pat Van Epps

CINNAMON ROLLS

½ cup vegetable shortening
1 cup milk
½ cup sugar
¾ teaspoon salt
1 (¼ ounce) package of dry
  yeast
3 eggs, beaten

6 cups all purpose flour, sifted
½ cup butter, softened
3 teaspoons cinnamon
3 teaspoons sugar
½ cup raisins
½ cup pecans, finely chopped

Scald shortening, milk, sugar and salt. Add yeast immediately. Cool. Add eggs and flour. Mix well. Place in large bowl, cover with a wet towel. Let rise 2 hours. Divide dough into two batches. Roll dough very thin. Spread with mxiture of softened butter, cinnamon, sugar, raisins, and pecans. Roll dough into long roll. Cut in ¾ inch slices. Place in greased pan. Let rise 2 hours. Preheat oven to 350 degrees. Bake for 15-18 minutes. Glaze.

Glaze for Cinnamon Rolls
½ cup melted butter
1½ cups powdered sugar

½-¾ cup milk

Cook to the consistency of syrup. Spread glaze over warm rolls.

Violet Pope

EASY ROLLS

3 cups flour
1 teaspoon baking powder
2 tablespoons sugar
2 teaspoons salt
2 packages active dry yeast

¼ cup water, warm
1 egg, well beaten
1 cup milk, warm
½ cup shortening
½ cup margarine, melted

Combine flour, baking powder, sugar and salt. Dissolve yeast in warm water. Add beaten egg to warm milk. Mix shortening well into the flour mixture. Pour in yeast mixture and milk mixture and mix well to make a soft dough. Let rise for 10 to 15 minutes. Roll out and cut as biscuits. Dip in melted margarine. Place on a pan and let rise to double size. Preheat oven to 375 degrees. Bake for 15 to 20 minutes.

Katie Ragsdale

DINNER ROLLS

¼ cup sugar
1 teaspoon salt
¼ cup margarine
1 cup milk, scalded

2 packages active dry yeast
½ cup water, warmed to 105 to
    115 degrees
2 eggs, beaten
5¼ cups bread flour (no
    substitute)

Add sugar, salt and margarine to scalded milk and stir until margarine is dissolved. Cool mixture until lukewarm. Dissolve yeast in warm water. Combine milk mixture, dissolved yeast, eggs and 2 cups flour. Beat until smooth. Add remaining flour gradually to make a soft dough. Turn dough onto lightly floured pastry cloth and knead until smooth and elastic. Bubbles will break under the surface after 10 to 12 minutes of kneading. Place in a greased bowl and turn once to grease the surface. Cover with a towel and let rise in a warm place until doubled in size. Punch down the dough and turn onto a lightly floured surface. Divide the dough into 3 equal pieces. Form each piece of the dough using one of the following methods. *Crescents:* Roll one piece of dough into a 12 inch circle with a rolling pin. Cut the circle into 12 to 16 triangles. Starting with the wide end, roll up the triangles and place point down on a greased cookie sheet. Cover and let rise until doubled in size. Preheat oven to 400 degrees. Brush with melted butter or margarine and bake for 12 minutes. *Pan Rolls:* Cut 1 piece of the dough into 9 equal parts. Roll each into a smooth ball and arrange in a greased cake pan. Cover and let rise until doubled in size. Preheat oven to 375 degrees. Brush with melted butter or margarine. Bake 15 to 18 minutes.*Cloverleaf Rolls:*Divide 1 piece of the dough into 27 equal pieces. Form each piece into a small ball. Place 3 balls in each section of a greased muffin pan. Cover and let rise until doubled in size. Preheat oven to 400 degrees. Brush with melted butter or margarine. Bake for 15 minutes.

Note: For a soft surface after baking, brush tops of the rolls with melted margarine. After the rolls are cooled on a wire rack, they can be wrapped and frozen. This saves time as the rolls are always ready. They are also low in cost when compared to those available in the stores, to say nothing of the taste and smell!

Shirley F. Burd

HOMEMAKER ROLLS

1 cake yeast
2 cups water, warm, divided
½ cup sugar

½ teaspoon salt
½ cup shortening, melted
5½ cups flour, sifted

Dissolve yeast in ½ cup warm water. Put sugar, salt and remaining warm water in a large mixing bowl. Pour melted shortening into water and sugar mixture. Add dissolved yeast mixture and 3 cups sifted flour; blend well. Cover bowl with cloth and sit in warm place to rise until doubled in size. Stir dough down with spoon. Add remaining 2½ cups flour slowly; work in until dough is just stiff enough to knead. Knead on lightly floured board until dough is smooth and elastic. Roll dough out and cut into rounds, or form into your favorite shape. Cover and let rise until doubled in size. Preheat oven to 450 degrees. Bake for 15 minutes.

Note: This dough keeps well in the refrigerator for up to a week. When refrigerated, pinch off dough as needed, form rolls, let rise and bake.

Nell Pewitt

HOT BEER ROLLS

½ cup beer
1 package active dry yeast
4 tablespoons margarine,
   melted and divided
½ cup evaporated milk,
   undiluted

1 tablespoon sugar
1 teaspoon salt
2½ cups flour

Heat beer until warm and put into mixing bowl. Sprinkle with the yeast and let stand until softened. Stir in 2 tablespoons margarine and remaining ingredients; mix well. Turn out on lightly floured pastry board or cloth and knead until smooth and elastic. Put into greased bowl and turn greased side of dough up. Cover and let rise in warm place 1 hour or until doubled in size. Punch down and cut into 12 pieces. Shape into balls and put into greased 2¾ inch muffin cups. Brush with remainder of melted margarine and let rise 30 minutes or until light. Bake at 425 degrees about 10 minutes. Makes 12 muffins.

Note: Dough can rise and be baked in a loaf pan.

June Ward

HOT CROSS BUNS

1 cup butter or margarine
1 cup sugar
2 cups milk, scalded
3 packages active dry yeast
2 large eggs
5 cups bread flour

3 cups whole wheat flour
½ teaspoon salt
1 teaspoon nutmeg
2 cups currants
⅓ to ½ cup candied citron

Put butter and sugar in *large* mixing bowl. Add scalded milk and stir until sugar is dissolved and butter is melted. Cool mixture to lukewarm (105 to 115 degrees) and then add the yeast. Stir to dissolve; add eggs and mix well. Sift the flours, salt and nutmeg together. Put currants and citron into a bowl; add several tablespoons of the flour mixture. Stir until fruits are coated. Add remainder of the flour gradually to the milk mixture, mixing well. Mix in the floured fruit. Knead dough thoroughly, 10-12 minutes. Place in a buttered bowl, turning once to butter the top. Cover with a damp towel and let rise until dough is doubled in size. Punch the dough down several times and turn onto a floured pastry cloth. Preheat oven to 375 degrees. Shape into 30 to 40 buns and place on a buttered cookie tin. Press a cross into each bun using a spatula. Bake for 10 minutes, reduce oven temperature to 350 degrees and bake for 10 to 15 minutes longer. When cool, frost along the lines fo the cross with frosting.

Note: Do not substitute regular soft wheat flours for the hard wheat, high gluten flours in the recipe.

Frosting:
2 tablespoons milk or water
1 cup powdered sugar

½ teaspoon vanilla

Stir the sugar gradually into the milk or water. Add vanilla and stir well. More sugar may be added if the frosting is not thick enough.

Shirley F. Burd

LOUISE'S ROLLS

2 packages active dry yeast
1 cup water, warm
1 cup vegetable shortening
¾ cup sugar

1 cup water, boiling
2 eggs, beaten
1 tablespoon salt
7½ cups flour

Dissolve yeast in lukewarm water. Cream shortening and add sugar; blend well. Add boiling water and stir to mix. Let cool to lukewarm. Add eggs and yeast; mix. Sift flour and salt together, add to yeast mixture in 2 additions; blend well after each addition. Cover and let rise in a warm place for 2 hours. Pinch off dough and roll to form rolls. Preheat oven to 450 degrees. Bake for 15 to 20 minutes.

Note: Dough may be refrigerated for several days. Pinch off dough and bake as needed.

Margaret Jenkins

PECAN POPOVERS WITH LEMON HONEY BUTTER

2 eggs
1 cup milk
½ teaspoon salt

1 cup flour
3 tablespoons pecans, finely
    chopped

Preheat oven to 425 degrees. Beat eggs, milk and salt together with wire whisk. Add flour; beat until smooth. Stir in pecans. Pour into 6 well-greased 5 or 6 ounce custard cups. Bake until puffed and golden brown 30-35 minutes. While popovers are baking make the Lemon Honey Butter.

Lemon Honey Butter
6 tablespoons butter, softened
6 tablespoons honey

¾ teaspoon grated lemon peel

Mix softened butter, honey and lemon peel together. Spread on warm popovers.

The Committee

REFRIGERATOR ROLLS I

1 package active dry yeast   ½ cup sugar
¼ cup water, warm   1 tablespoon salt
2 cups milk, scalded   2 egg whites, beaten
½ cup shortening   6½ cups flour

Dissolve yeast in warm water (110-115 degrees). In mixing bowl, stir scalded milk, shortening and sugar until dissolved. Cool to lukewarm. Add yeast mixture and salt; stir and blend in egg whites. Add flour in 2 to 3 additions and mix after each addition until smooth. Cover and let rise in warm place for about an hour or until doubled in size. Punch down and refrigerate in covered container. Take out enough dough for each use. Shape into rolls and let rise for 1 hour. Bake at 400 degrees for 10 to 15 minutes.

Note: For cloverleaf rolls, make 1 inch balls of dough and place 3 in each greased muffin cup.

Jo Pool

REFRIGERATOR ROLLS II

6 tablespoons shortening   ¼ cup water, warm
¼ cup sugar   1 egg
1 teaspoon salt   3½ cups sifted flour
1 cup milk, scalded   butter, melted
1 package active dry yeast

In a large bowl, combine shortening, sugar and salt. Stir in milk until shortening and sugar are melted. Dissolve yeast in warm water. After the first mixture cools, beat in the egg and dissolved yeast. Add flour. Place in the refrigerator immediately and leave about ½ day. About 1½ hours before baking, roll out dough on a floured board. Work in just enough flour to keep from sticking and roll out until dough is just under ½ inch thick. Cut circles with biscuit cutter. Dab top of each with melted butter, fold in half and place side by side in a well greased pan. Brush tops lightly with melted butter. Cover with a towel and let rise. Preheat oven to 400 degrees. Bake until golden brown (about 15 minutes.)

Linda White

REFRIGERATOR ROLLS III

1¾ cups water, hot
½ cup sugar
1 tablespoon salt
3 tablespoons margarine
2 packages active dry yeast

1 egg, beaten
5¼ cups unsifted *bread* flour
  (no substitution)
¼ cup butter or margarine,
  melted

Mix together water, sugar, salt and margarine. Stir until margarine is melted. Cool to lukewarm (105-115 degrees). Sprinkle in the yeast and add the egg. Beat well. Add half the flour. Beat well. Stir in the remaining flour. Turn the dough onto a floured pastry cloth. Knead until the dough is smooth, elastic and small bubbles form under the surface of the dough. The kneading takes about 12 to 15 minutes. Grease a large bowl. Place the dough in the bowl and turn once so that all the surface is greased. Cover with foil and store in the refrigerator until the dough doubles in size (usually overnight.). May be stored in the refrigerator for 4 to 5 days. When using, punch dough down and take out desired amount. Form into desired shape. Place in a greased pan, cover with a towel and let rise until doubled in size. Preheat oven to 375 degrees. Brush with melted margarine and bake for 15 to 20 minutes (pan rolls), or at 400 degrees for 15 minutes for cloverleaf rolls. Makes 27 rolls.

Note: To make cloverleaf rolls, use a muffin tin. Divide dough for each roll into three parts. Shape each part into a small ball.

Shirley F. Burd

SPOON BREAD

1 cup white corn meal
¾ cup water, boiling
1 teaspoon salt
1½ teaspoons sugar

1 large egg, beaten
½ teaspoon soda
1 cup buttermilk
1½ tablespoons butter, melted

Preheat oven to 375 degrees. Place corn meal in a bowl. Pour the boiling water over it and stir well. Cover and cool. Then, add salt, sugar and egg. Dissolve soda in the buttermilk and add to corn meal mixture, mixing well. Add butter; mix again. Bake in greased souffle dish or greased iron skillet for 30 to 35 minutes. Serve immediately!

Shirley F. Burd

HUSH PUPPIES

2 cups white corn meal
1 tablespoon flour
½ teaspoon soda
1 teaspoon baking powder
2 teaspoons sugar

1½ teaspoon salt
1 cup buttermilk
1 small onion, finely chopped
   (optional)
1 egg, beaten

Mix all ingredients together, adding egg last. Drop from a teaspoon into deep hot fat. Hush Puppies will float to the surface of the fat and turn golden brown. When done, dip out with a slotted spoon and drain on paper towels.

Joyce Montgomery

Cakes and Frostings

ANGEL CAKE SUPREME

1 (3¾ ounce) package lemon pudding and pie filling mix
2 tablespoons lemon juice
1 tablespoon lemon peel, grated
1 cup heavy cream

1 (3½ ounce) can flaked coconut
1 angel food cake, split into 2 layers

Prepare pudding, using only 2 cups of water and cook until thick. Stir in lemon juice and grated peel; allow to cool. Whip cream and mix with coconut. Fold into pudding: spread cream and pudding mixture between layers of angel food cake. Refrigerate overnight.

Topping for Angel Cake Supreme
1½ cups heavy cream
2 tablespoons powdered sugar, if desired

1 (3½ ounce) can flaked coconut.

Shortly before serving cake, whip the cream adding sugar when cream begins to thicken. Spread over top and sides of cake and sprinkle with coconut.

Nancy Cannon

APRICOT NECTAR CAKE

1 (18½ ounce) package lemon cake mix
4 eggs

½ cup sugar
¾ cup vegetable oil
1 cup apricot nectar

Combine all ingredients in a large mixing bowl. Beat with electric mixer for 2 minutes. Bake in greased and floured 8x11 inch baking pan at 350 degrees for one hour.

Lemon Juice Glaze
1½ cups powdered sugar

6 tablespoons lemon juice

Blend powdered sugar and lemon juice until smooth. Spread on cake after cake has cooled slightly and is still warm but not hot.

Betty Jo Walker

"MY" BIRTHDAY CAKE

1⅓ cups cooked prunes,
   drained
2½ cups cake flour, sifted
1 teaspoon salt
1½ teaspoon cinnamon
¼ teaspoon nutmeg
1 teaspoon baking soda
½ cup milk

1 cup sugar, divided
⅔ cup vegetable shortening
3 large eggs, separated
1 teaspoon vanilla
½ to ¾ cup black walnuts, cut
   up

Chop prunes finely and reserve. Sift flour, salt, cinnamon and nutmeg together 2 or 3 times and reserve. Stir baking soda into milk and reserve. Separate out 3 to 3½ tablespoons of the sugar and reserve. Cream shortening with remaining sugar. Reserve egg whites. Add egg yolks to shortening and sugar mixture. Beat thoroughly. Add the sifted ingredients alternately with milk and baking soda mixture. Beat well after each addition. Add vanilla, chopped prunes, and cut walnuts to batter, mixing well. In separate bowl, beat egg whites until almost stiff. Add the 3 - 3½ tablespoons sugar to egg whites and continue beating until stiff. Fold egg whites into the batter. Pour into layer pans. Bake in a 375 degree oven for 30 to 33 minutes. Frost with Butter Frosting or seven minute frosting.

Butter Frosting
4 tablespoons butter or
   margarine
1½ teaspoons vanilla

1 (16 ounce) box powdered
   sugar
milk

Soften butter to room temperature. Using hand mixer, blend in vanilla and sugar. Add milk by tablespoons until the icing is of desired spreading consistency. Sufficient for top, center, and sides of a two layer cake.

Katherine Horton Farley

BANANA CRUNCH CAKE

2½ tablespoons butter or
  margarine
½ (7½ ounce) package coconut
  pecan frosting mix or
  (8¼ ounce) package coconut
  almond frosting mix

½ cup rolled oats
1 cup commerical sour cream
4 eggs
2 large bananas, mashed
1 (17 ounce) package yellow
  cake mix

Grease and flour a 10 inch tube pan. Melt butter in sauce pan; stir in frosting mix and oats until crumbly; set aside. Blend in sour cream, eggs, and bananas in a large bowl until smooth. Blend in cake mix; beat 2 minutes at medium speed on regular electric mixer (higher speed with portable mixer). Pour one-third of batter (2 cups) into prepared pan. Sprinkle with one-third of crumb mixture (one-half cup). Repeat twice with batter and crumb mixture, ending with crumb mixture. Bake in a preheated 350 degree oven for 50 to 60 minutes. Turn pan upside down on cake rack; then turn cake so crumb mixture is on top.

Lucy Campbell

CHIP AND CHERRY CAKE
(BISHOPS' CAKE)

3 eggs
1 cup sugar
1½ cups flour, sifted
1½ teaspoons baking powder
¼ teaspoon salt

¾ cup chocolate chips
2 cups pecans, coarsely
  chopped
1 cup dates, chopped
1 cup candied cherries, halved

Beat eggs for 5 minutes. Add sugar and beat 4 more minutes. Sift flour, baking powder and salt together. Add to egg and sugar mixture and mix well. Fold chips, pecan, dates and cherries into batter. Line a 9x5x3 inch loaf pan with waxed paper and oil the waxed paper. Bake at 325 degrees for 1½ hours. Turn out of pan, remove waxed paper and cool.

Isabelle Friedberg

CARROT CAKE

2½ cups flour
2½ teaspoons cinnamon
1½ teaspoons baking soda
½ teaspoon salt
½ cup vegetable oil
2 cups sugar

4 egg yolks
3½ tablespoons hot water
1½ cups carrots, grated
1 cup nuts, chopped
4 egg whites, beaten

Sift together flour, cinnamon, soda and salt. Set aside. Combine oil, sugar, egg yolks, water and carrots using low speed of electric mixer. Add sifted ingredients, mixing thoroughly. Blend in nuts, then fold in egg whites. Bake in a greased tube pan at 300 degrees for at least an hour. Test for doneness. Frost with Brown Sugar Frosting.

Brown Sugar Frosting
1 cup light brown sugar
½ cup margarine

⅓ cup milk
2 cups powdered sugar, sifted

In a saucepan beat brown sugar, margarine and milk. Boil and stir 2 minutes. Cool for 30 minutes. Gradually add sugar and mix until smooth and of spreading consistency.

Note: Add more sugar to thicken or more milk to thin.

Dorothy Griscom

COCONUT SOUR CREAM LAYER CAKE

1 package butter- flavor cake
  mix
2 cups sugar
1 (16 ounce) carton sour cream

1 (12 ounce) package frozen
  coconut, thawed
1½ cups frozen whipped
  topping,thawed

Prepare cake mix and bake in 2 layers. When cool, split both layers. Combine sugar, sour cream and coconut, blending well. Chill. Reserve 1 cup for frosting, spread remainder between layers. Combine reserved sour cream mix with whipped topping, blend until smooth. Cover sides and top of cake with this mixture. Seal in air tight container and refrigerate for 3 days before serving.

Margaret Jenkins

ORANGE COCONUT CAKE

¾ cup vegetable shortening
¾ teaspoon salt
rind of one orange, grated
1½ cups sugar
3 eggs, unbeaten
3 cups cake flour, sifted
3 teaspoons baking powder

juice of one orange
2 tablespoons lemon juice
water
1½ cups of coconut, rubbed
together with grated rind of
one orange

Grease two deep 9 inch layer pans and dust with flour. Combine shortening, salt and grated orange rind. Add sugar gradually and cream the mixture until light and fluffy. Add eggs, one at a time, beating thoroughly after each addition. Sift flour and baking powder together 3 times. Combine orange juice and lemon juice: add water to make one cup of fluid. Alternately, add flour in small amounts with the combined juices and water, beating well after each addition. Pour batter into the cake pans. Bake in a preheated 375 degree oven for 25 to 30 minutes. After cooling the layers, spread with a boiled frosting between layers and over top and sides. Sprinkle with orange flavored coconut while frosting is soft.

Boiled Frosting
1½ cups sugar
½ teaspoon light corn syrup
½ cup water, boiling

2 egg whites, stiffly beaten
1 teaspoon vanilla or orange
flavoring

Combine, sugar, corn syrup and boiling water in a heavy saucepan and cook until the mixture spins a long thread (240F. degrees on candy thermometer). Pour syrup slowly over egg whites beating constantly. Add flavoring and continue beating until the mixture is cool and stiff enough to hold its shape. Frosts two 9 inch cake layers.

Note: It is better not to try this on a hot, humid day.

Katherine Horton Farley

COCONUT SHEET CAKE

1 (18½ ounce) package white cake mix
1 (14 ounce) can sweetened condensed milk
1 (8 ounce) can coconut milk
1 (12 ounce) carton Cool Whip
2 to 3 (12 ounce) packages frozen coconut
1 cup nuts, chopped, (optional)

Prepare cake following package directions and bake in a 9x13 inch pan. Mix sweetened condensed milk and coconut milk; drizzle over hot cake. When cake is cool, spread Cool Whip over cake and sprinkle with coconut. Sprinkle nuts over coconut if desired. Refrigerate overnight.

Margaret Jenkins

SOUR CREAM COCONUT CAKE

1 box Duncan Hines Yellow Cake Mix (Deluxe II)

TOPPING:
1 (8 ounce) carton Cool Whip
1 (8 ounce) sour cream
2 (6 ounce) packages frozen coconut
½ cup sugar

Bake cake in 2 layers as directed on package. Cool, then split into 4 layers. Combine topping ingredients and mix well. Spread between layers, on sides and over top of cake. Store, tightly covered, in refrigerator for 4 days before serving.

Joan Dodson

CHOCOLATE CAKE

2 cups flour
¼ teaspoon salt
2 cups sugar
1 cup margarine
4 tablespoons cocoa

1 cup water
2 eggs
1 teaspoon vanilla
½ cup buttermilk
1 teaspoon soda

Sift together flour, salt, sugar. Set aside. Heat margarine, cocoa, and water in a saucepan and bring to a boil. Pour boiling liquid over dry mixture. Add eggs, vanilla, buttermilk and soda. Mix well. Pour into 13x9 inch sheet pan. Mixture will be thin. Bake in preheated 350 degree oven for 30-35 minutes.

COCOA ICING I
½ cup margarine
4 tablespoons cocoa
6 tablespoons milk
1 (16 ounce) box powdered
 sugar

1 teaspoon vanilla
1 cup nuts, chopped

Melt margarine and stir in cocoa and milk. Add sugar, vanilla, and nuts. Mix well. Pour over hot cake.

Pat Worley

MIRACLE WHIP CAKE

1 cup lukewarm water
1 cup Miracle Whip Salad
 Dressing
3 tablespoons cocoa
2 cups flour

1 cup sugar
2 teaspoons baking soda
⅛ teaspoon salt
2 teaspoons vanilla

Mix water and salad dressing. Blend in cocoa, flour, sugar, baking soda and salt. Add vanilla and mix thoroughly. Pour into 2 paper lined 9 inch cake pans and bake in 350 degree oven for 35 minutes. Frost with Cocoa Icing II.

Note: This cake becomes more moist as it sits.

Cocoa Icing II
1½ cups sugar
½ cup milk

3 tablespoons cocoa
¼ cup butter

Combine sugar, milk and cocoa in a saucepan and boil for 3 minutes. Add butter and boil for 3 more minutes. Beat until spreading consistency.

Margaret Jenkins

EGGLESS CHOCOLATE CAKE

3 cups flour,sifted
2 cups sugar
¼ cup cocoa
2 teaspoons soda
⅛ teaspoon salt

2 cups buttermilk
½ cup margarine
2 tablespoons salad oil
2 teaspoons vanilla

Sift flour, sugar, cocoa and salt together in a large bowl. Add buttermilk, margarine, salad oil and vanilla. Mix well and pour into cake pan. Bake in a preheated 350 degree oven 35-40 minutes for a 9x13 inch pan or 25-30 minutes for 2 round 8 inch pans.

Cocoa Frosting III
2 cups sugar
¼ cup cocoa
¼ teaspoon salt
8 tablespoons shortening

⅔ cup milk
2 teaspoons vanilla
½ cup nut meats (optional)

Combine sugar, cocoa, salt, shortening and milk in a sauce pan. Bring to a boil and cook for one minute. Remove from heat and add vanilla. Beat well. Stir in nuts if desired.

Carolyn M. Oxford

MOTHER-IN-LAW'S CHOCOLATE CAKE
(It's true, her's is better than mine!)

2 cups flour, sifted
½ teaspoon salt
1 teaspoon baking soda
½ cup vegetable shortening
1½ cups sugar

2 eggs
4 tablespoons cocoa
4 tablespoons coffee
1 teaspoon vanilla
1 cup sour milk

Sift the flour with the salt and baking soda and reserve. Grease and flour two 8 or 9 inch cake pans. In a large mixing bowl, cream shortening with the sugar. Add the eggs one at a time, beating well after each addition. Add the cocoa, coffee, and vanilla and beat well. Add flour mixture in small amounts alternating with small amounts of sour milk, beating well after each addition. Divide the batter between the two cake pans.

Note: When using 8 inch pans, I usually take out enough for three or four cupcakes (or 6 to 8 tea size cupcakes).

Bake at 350 degrees for 30-35 minutes, checking with a straw. (Cupcakes: 12-15 minutes). Place pans on a rack to cool for 5-10 minutes. Put a rack over the top of each layer and turn layers upside down. Remove pans to complete cooling. Frost with a butter icing. Enjoy!

Another note: If you do not have sour milk, you can use my substitute which is one cup of sweet milk plus one tablespoon white cider vinegar (5% acidity). Prepare this before you begin mixing other ingredients.

Sadie Walsh Burd

SOUR CREAM CHOCOLATE CAKE

3 cups cake flour, sifted
¼ teaspoon baking soda
½ cup cocoa
1 cup butter or margarine
3 cups sugar

6 eggs
1 cup sour cream
1 teaspoon vanilla, lemon or
   almond extract

Sift together flour, baking soda and cocoa. In a large mixing bowl cream butter and sugar, add eggs one at a time and beat well. Add sour cream in portions alternately with the flour mixture. Add flavoring extract. Bake in greased and floured tube pan at 300 degrees for 1½ hours. Cool and ice.

Butter Icing
1 cup butter
1 box (16 ounces) powdered
   sugar

1 teaspoon vanilla
¼ cup milk

Cream together butter, sugar and vanilla. Add enough milk to make of spreading consistency.

Leon S. McAulay

AUNT WILLIE'S FUDGE CAKE

1 cup butter
8 tablespoons cocoa
4 eggs
2 cups of sugar

1½ cups flour
1 teaspoon vanilla
1 cup pecans, chopped

Melt butter and cocoa over low heat while creaming eggs and sugar in bowl. Add hot chocolate mixture to eggs and sugar. Beat well. Add flour a little at a time, mixing well. Add vanilla and nuts. Spray an 8x12 inch pan with a vegetable spray shortening and pour in batter. Bake 25 to 30 minutes in a preheated 325 degree oven. Cool slightly before cutting.

Peggy Sparrenberger

ITALIAN CREAM CAKE

½ cup margarine
½ cup shortening or oil
2 cups sugar
5 egg yolks
2 cups flour, sifted
1 teaspoon baking powder

1 teaspoon baking soda
1 cup buttermilk
1 teaspoon vanilla
1⅓ cups flaked coconut
1 cup pecans, finely chopped
5 egg whites, stiffly beaten

Cream margarine, shortening and sugar. Beat until smooth. Add yolks one at a time, beating well after each addition. Sift flour, baking powder and soda together and add to batter alternately with buttermilk. Stir in vanilla, coconut and pecans. Gently fold in egg whites. Pour into a large loaf pan and bake at 350 degrees for 30-35 minutes. Cool completely before frosting with cream cheese frosting.

Cream Cheese Frosting
6 ounces cream cheese,
   softened
6 tablespoons butter, softened

12 ounces powdered sugar
¾ teaspoon vanilla
½ cup pecans, chopped

Whip cream cheese, butter and sugar until light and fluffy. Blend in vanilla. Spread over top of cake and sprinkle with nuts.

Jean Smith

FIG PRESERVE CAKE

2 cups flour
1 teaspoon baking soda
1 teaspoon salt
1 teaspoon ground nutmeg
½ teaspoon ground cloves
1 teaspoon cinnamon
1½ cups sugar

1 cup cooking oil
3 eggs
1 cup buttermilk
1 cup fig preserves, chopped
½ cup pecans, chopped
1 tablespoon vanilla

Grease and flour a bundt pan or 10 inch tube pan. Sift together flour, soda, salt and spices. Combine sugar, oil, eggs, and buttermilk in large mixing bowl and beat well. Add flour mixture and mix well. Add preserves, pecans and vanilla. Pour into prepared tube pan and bake 1 hour at 325 degrees. Pour Buttermilk Sauce over cake immediately after removing from oven.

Buttermilk Sauce

1 cup sugar	½ cup margarine
½ cup buttermilk	1 tablespoon white corn syrup
1 tablespoon vanilla	½ teaspoon baking soda

Mix all ingredients in sauce pan and boil for three minutes. Pour over cake as soon as it is removed from oven and still in pan. May be served with or without whipped cream or whipped topping.

Lucy Campbell

FRUIT COCKTAIL CAKE

2 cups flour	2 eggs
2 (13 ounce) cans fruit cocktail	1½ cups sugar
(undrained)	½ teaspoon salt

Mix all ingredients and beat 1 minute. Bake at 325 degrees for 45 minutes to 1 hour. Glaze with Coconut Icing.

Coconut Icing

¾ cup brown sugar	1 cup coconut
½ cup evaporated milk	1 teaspoon vanilla
½ cup margarine	

Combine sugar, milk and margarine in a sauce pan and bring to boil. Boil 2 minutes. Add coconut and vanilla. Pour over cool cake.

Pat Worley

MANDARIN ORANGE CAKE

1 (18 ounce) package yellow
   cake mix
4 eggs

½ cup vegetable oil
1 (11 ounce) can mandarin
   oranges, undrained

Combine all ingredients in a mixing bowl and beat for 2 minutes. Pour into a greased and floured 9x13 inch pan. Bake at 325 degrees for 25 to 35 minutes. Turn out on a large rectangular tray and cool before frosting with Pineapple Topping.

Pineapple Topping
1 (8 ounce) package Cool Whip
1 (3¾ ounce) package instant
   vanilla pudding (dry from
   package)

1 (20 ounce) can crushed
   pineapple, drained

Combine all ingredients, mix well for 3 minutes. Spread over top and sides of cake. Chill and serve.

Dianna Thompson

NAMELESS CAKE

1 (3 ounce) package lemon
   gelatin
¾ cup water, boiling
1 package (18 ounce) yellow
   cake mix

¾ cup vegetable oil
1 teaspoon lemon juice, fresh
4 eggs

Dissolve gelatin in boiling water. Combine cake mix and vegetable oil. Add lemon juice and eggs. Beat well. Blend in gelatin. Bake at 350 degrees in a greased and floured tube or bundt pan for 35-45 minutes. Glaze with Orange Topping.

Orange Topping
¾ cup orange juice
½ cup granulated sugar

4 tablespoons powdered sugar

Prepare glaze by mixing orange juice and granulated sugar. As soon as cake is out of oven, turn onto cake plate. Make random holes with a toothpick. Sprinkle powdered sugar over cake. Slowly pour orange mixture over cake or brush cake with mixture using pastry brush.

Patricia D. Hallmark

NUTTY CAKE

1 (29 ounce) can sliced
  peaches, undrained
1 (17 ounce) package butter
  pecan cake mix

½ cup margarine or butter
½ cup coconut
½ cup pecans, chopped
Cool Whip

In a 1½ quart flat baking dish, place peaches, juice and all. Sprinkle dry cake mix over peaches. Melt margarine. Pour over cake and mix evenly. Sprinkle coconut and pecans on top. Bake at 350 degrees for 40 minutes. Serve with Cool Whip on top.

Armatine Keller

OLD FASHIONED POUND CAKE

1¾ cups margarine
2 cups sugar
6 eggs

1 tablespoon vanilla extract
1 tablespoon lemon extract
3 cups flour

Cream margarine, add sugar and cream well. Add eggs one at a time and beat well. Add extracts, mix in flour, ½ cup at a time, and cream well. Mixing well after each addition is very important for a light textured cake. Pour into a greased and floured tube pan. Place cake in a cold oven and turn on to 300 degrees. Bake 1 hour and 55 minutes, or longer if necessary.

The Committee

CREAM CHEESE POUND CAKE

1½ cups butter
1 (8 ounce) package cream
  cheese
3 cups sugar

6 eggs
1 teaspoon vanilla
3 cups flour, sifted

Cream together butter, cheese and sugar. Add eggs, one at a time, beating after each one. Add vanilla. Add flour slowly while beating. Beat batter for 5 minutes on high speed. Pour into greased and floured Bundt pan or 10x4 inch tube pan. Place in cold oven, turn to 300 degrees and bake for 1½ hours.

Zinnie Bueno

GOOEY BUTTER CAKE

1 (18 ounce) box pound cake
 mix
½ cup margarine, melted
2 eggs
1 (8 ounce) package cream
 cheese

1 (16 ounce) box powdered
 sugar
2 eggs

Prepare cake mix with margarine and 2 eggs. Spread in a 9x13 inch pan. Beat cream cheese, powdered sugar and 2 eggs together and spread on top of batter. Sprinkle top with powdered sugar and bake in a preheated 350 degree oven for 35 minutes.

Mary Pat Van Epps

PUMPKIN CAKE

2 cups flour
2 cups sugar
2 teaspoons baking powder
2 teaspoons baking soda
2 teaspoons cinnamon

1 teaspoon salt
1 (14 ounce) can pumpkin
1¼ cups oil
1 teaspoon vanilla
½ teaspoon nutmeg

Sift flour, sugar, baking powder, soda, cinnamon and salt together. Add pumpkin, oil and vanilla. Mix well. Add nutmeg. Pour into a 9x13 inch pan and bake in 350 degree oven for 1 hour. Frost with Cream Cheese Icing.

Cream Cheese Icing
½ cup margarine
1 (8 ounce) package cream
 cheese
2 tablespoons milk

2 teaspoons vanilla
1 (1 pound) box powdered
 sugar

Combine margarine and cheese and beat. Add milk and continue beating. Blend in vanilla and sugar and mix well. Spread over cake.

Pat Worley

PIÑA COLADA PUDDING CAKE

1 (18½ ounce) white cake mix
1 (3⅓ ounce) package coconut
   cream or vanilla instant
   pudding

4 eggs
½ cup water
⅓ cup dark rum
¼ cup vegetable oil

Note: If using vanilla instant pudding, increase water to ¾ cup and add 1 cup flaked coconut to the batter.

Blend cake mix, pudding mix, eggs, water, rum and oil in a large mixer bowl. Beat 4 minutes at medium speed of electric mixer. Pour into 2 greased and floured 9 inch cake pans. Bake in a preheated 350 degree oven for 25 to 30 minutes or until cake springs back when lightly pressed or when cake begins to pull away from the sides of the pans. Do not underbake. Cool in pans for 15 minutes; remove and finish cooling on racks.

Note: In high altitudes, use three large eggs and add 2 tablespoons all purpose flour and increase water to 1 cup (1¼ cups with vanilla instant pudding); beat 2 minutes and bake 30 minutes.

Piña Colada Frosting
1 (8 ounce) can crushed
   pineapple in juice
1 (3⅛ ounce) package coconut
   cream or vanilla instant
   pudding

⅓ cup dark rum
1 (9 ounce) carton Cool Whip,
   thawed
1 cup flaked coconut

Combine pineapple, pudding mix, and rum in a bowl; beat until well blended. Fold in Cool Whip. Fill and frost cakes with this mixture; sprinkle with coconut. Chill. Refrigerate any left over cake.

Kathy Minner

THREE FLAVOR CAKE

½ cup butter
½ cup shortening
3 cups sugar
5 eggs
3 cups flour

1 cup milk
½ teaspoon baking powder
1 teaspoon coconut flavoring
1 teaspoon butter flavoring
1 teaspoon rum flavoring

Mix butter, shortening and sugar. Add eggs and beat. Add flour and milk, beat. Stir in baking powder and flavorings. Bake in a Bundt pan at 325 degrees fo 1½ hours.

Three Flavor Cake Glaze
½ cup sugar
¼ cup water
1 teaspoon coconut flavoring

1 teaspoon butter flavoring
1 teaspoon rum flavoring
½ teaspoon almond flavoring

Combine and pour over cake while hot.

Margaret Jenkins

YUM-YUM CAKE

2 cups flour, sifted
2 teaspoons soda
1 teaspoon vanilla
2 cups sugar

2 eggs, slightly beaten
¼ teaspoon salt
1 (20 ounce) can crushed
    pineapple

Combine all ingredients in large bowl. Mix by hand. Bake in greased and floured 9x13 inch pan at 350 degrees for 30 minutes. Remove from oven and while cake is still hot spread with Coconut Topping.

Coconut Topping
1 cup sugar
1 (5½ ounce) can evaporated
    milk
½ cup butter or margarine

3 tablespoons flour
1 cup flaked or grated coconut
1 cup nut meats, chopped

Combine sugar, milk, margarine and flour in a sauce pan and cook over low heat until slightly thickened. Stir in coconut and nut meats. Spread over hot cake.

Kathy Scott

Cookies and Candies

ALMOND COOKIES

½ cup butter
½ cup shortening
½ cup white sugar
½ cup brown sugar
1 egg, beaten
½ cup almonds, ground

1 teaspoon almond extract
2½ cups flour
1½ teaspoons baking powder
½ teaspoon salt
4-5 dozen almond halves

Glaze
1 egg yolk
1 tablespoon water

2 drops each of red and yellow
  food coloring

Cream butter, shortening and sugars. Blend in egg, almonds and extract. Sift together flour, baking powder and salt. Blend into egg mixture. Dough will be stiff. Shape into 1 inch balls. Place 2 inches apart on greased cookie sheets. Press almond half on each ball and flatten to ½ inch thickness. Make glaze by mixing egg yolk, water and food coloring. Brush on each cookie. Preheat oven to 350 degrees. Bake 10-13 minutes or until lightly browned. Let cool on sheets before removing to prevent crumbling. Makes 4-5 dozen.

Tine Keller

ALMOND MACAROONS

8 egg whites
2½ cups sugar
1 teaspoon almond extract
1 pound blanched almonds,
  grated

½ pound blanched almonds,
  whole

Beat egg whites until foamy. Add the sugar, two tablespoons at a time, over a 30 minute period. Add extract and grated almonds. Refrigerate for two hours. Line cookie sheet with brown paper (unglazed). Drop dough onto brown paper by the teaspoonful. Place (press) a whole almond into each macaroon's center. Let stand overnight. Preheat oven to 300 degrees. Bake for one hour or until cookies can be lifted from the paper. Place on cooling racks.

Note: These can be frozen and thawed for later use.

Shirley F. Burd

ALMOND TOFFEE BARS

1 box graham crackers
1 (2¾ ounce) package sliced
   almonds

½ cup butter (NO SUBSTITUTE)
½ cup margarine
½ cup sugar

Separate graham crackers into fourths and place in a 9x13 inch pan to cover the bottom. Sprinkle almonds on top of graham crackers. In a saucepan, gently melt the butter and margarine and gradually add the sugar. Stir constantly with a wooden spoon and cook over medium high heat until mixture begins to boil. Boil for 2 minutes. Pour over graham crackers and almonds and spread evenly. Bake at 325 degrees for 12 minutes. Remove from oven and let stand 15 minutes. Cut around crackers and lift out.

Mary Pat Van Epps

APPLESAUCE BARS

½ cup butter
1½ cups sugar
1½ cups applesauce
1 teaspoon cinnamon
1 teaspoon salt
2 teaspoons baking soda

2¼ cups flour
½ cup nuts, chopped
1 cup raisins
2 cups powdered sugar
2-3 tablespoons lemon juice, or
   more

Cream butter and sugar together until light and fluffy. Stir in applesauce. Add cinnamon, salt, soda, and flour and mix well. Stir in nuts and raisins. Pour into well greased 9x13 inch pan and bake at 375 degrees for 25-30 minutes. Moisten the powdered sugar with the lemon juice and spread over the hot baked mixture. Cool in pan and cut into bars.

Mary Pat Van Epps

DOUBLE FROSTED BROWNIES

1 cup margarine
2 cups sugar
4 squares bitter chocolate,
   melted
4 eggs

2 cups nuts, chopped
1 cup flour
1 teaspoon vanilla
½ teaspoon salt

Cream margarine and sugar, then blend in chocolate. Add eggs one at a time and mix well. Add nuts, flour, vanilla and salt. Spread in a 10x15 inch pan. Bake at 350 degrees for 20 minutes. Cool.

Frosting
¼ cup butter
3 cups powdered sugar
5 tablespoons cream or
   evaporated milk

1 teaspoon vanilla

Cream butter and sugar together, add cream or evaporated milk and vanilla. Spread over brownies.

Glaze
2 squares bitter chocolate

2 tablespoons butter

Melt chocolate and butter together. Cool. Dribble over frosted brownies. Store in refrigerator until cool. Cut into squares. Keeps indefinitely in airtight container.

Mary Gowen

FRENCH MELT-A-WAY COOKIES

¾ cup corn starch, unsifted
1 cup flour

½ pound butter
½ cup powdered sugar

Mix cookie ingredients and chill. Preheat oven to 350 degrees. When dough is thoroughly chilled, form into small balls, place on baking sheet and flatten with a fork. Bake for 12 minutes. Cool on baking sheet before removing. Handle gently as cookies are very short. Makes 60 small cookies.

Frosting

3 ounces cream cheese   **½ cup powdered sugar**

Mix ingredients well and pipe from pastry bag with tip onto cookie centers. May also be spread.

Note: This recipe can be made in seconds in the food processor.

Nancy Willis

CHRISTMAS BUTTER COOKIES

2 cups butter, softened   **1 egg**
1 cup sugar   **4½ cups sifted flour**
2 teaspoons vanilla

Cream butter and sugar until fluffy and light. Blend in the vanilla and egg. Blend in flour. Cover and refrigerate for a minimum of 2 hours. Roll out ¼ of the dough, refrigerating the remainder. Roll to ⅛ inch thick and cut out with Christmas cookie cutters and put on ungreased cookie sheet. (If being used for Christmas tree decorations make a hole in each cookie with a skewer). Brush those that are not to be iced with glaze. Preheat oven to 375 degrees. Bake for 6-8 minutes until edges are lightly browned. Cool for 1-2 minutes and remove from sheet. Decorate the unglazed cookies with icing and hang on the tree!

Glaze
1 egg yolk   **1 tablespoon water**

Mix together and brush onto cookies before cooking.

Icing
2 egg whites   **3 cups powdered sugar**
¼ teaspoon cream of tartar   **2 teaspoons vanilla**
⅛ teaspoon salt   **food coloring**

Beat egg whites, cream of tartar and salt until stiff (not dry). Stir in the sugar and beat to shiny peaks (not stiff) and blend in vanilla. Place in small dishes to add the desired color of food coloring - red, green, blue, yellow needed to make the Christmas designs on the butter cookies.

Shirley F. Burd

BUTTERSCOTCH SQUARES

1 (16 ounce) package brown
  sugar
4 eggs, beaten
1 cup pecans, chopped
2 cups flour, sifted

1 teaspoon baking powder
pinch of salt
juice of ½ orange
powdered sugar

Beat brown sugar and eggs together. Pour into double boiler and cook for 20 minutes. Stir constantly while cooking. Combine pecans, flour, baking powder and salt. Stir this combination into cooked brown sugar and eggs. Add the juice of ½ of an orange for flavor. Pour into well-greased 8x8 inch baking pan. Bake for 15 minutes. Allow to cool. Cut into squares before removing from pan. Roll squares in powdered sugar.

Martha Risner

WHITE CHRISTMAS BALLS (DATE-NUT BALLS)

1 cup butter
1 cup sugar
1 pound pitted dates
1 cup pecans, chopped

2 cups crispy rice cereal
1 teaspoon vanilla
powdered sugar

Mix butter, sugar and dates in heavy skillet and cook over very low heat until butter is absorbed. Stir frequently. Then, add pecans, rice cereal and vanilla. Mix until fairly evenly distributed. Let mixture cool until it is handling temperature, then roll into 1 inch balls. When balls are cool, roll them in powdered sugar. Makes 75-100 balls. Store in covered container or freeze if long-term storage is desired.

Candy Vine

CHRISTMAS COOKIES

1 cup vegetable oil or
    shortening
2 cups brown sugar
3 eggs
3 cups flour
½ teaspoon salt
1 teaspoon soda
2 teaspoons cinnamon

½ teaspoon cloves
½ teaspoon allspice
½ teaspoon nutmeg
½ teaspoon ginger
½ cup milk or less
3 pounds chopped dates
1½ pounds chopped nuts

Preheat oven to 375 degrees. Cream shortening and sugar. Add eggs, one at a time. Sift flour, salt, soda, and spices together. Add to creamed mixture, alternating with milk. By hand, stir in dates and nuts. Drop by spoonful onto ungreased cookie sheet. Bake for 10-12 minutes.

Mamie Radar

CREAM CHEESE COOKIES

1 (8 ounce) package cream
    cheese, softened
½ cup butter or margarine
½ cup shortening

1 cup sugar
2 cups flour
1 teaspoon vanilla
dash of salt

In mixing bowl cream together cheese, butter, shortening and sugar. Add flour, vanilla, and salt and mix well. Chill the dough for at least 2 hours. Dough can be tinted. Put through a cookie press or drop from spoon on greased cookie sheet. Bake at 400 degrees for 8-10 minutes. Makes 4-5 dozen.

Tine Keller

COCONUT DATE BARS

½ cup butter, softened
¼ cup brown sugar
1½ cups granulated sugar
3 eggs
2½ cups all purpose flour

½ cup milk
¼ cup lemon juice
1 cup dates, chopped
1 cup coconut, flaked

Cream together butter and sugars. Add eggs and beat well. Add flour and milk, a little at a time, alternately. Mix well. Add lemon juice and beat well. Stir in dates and coconut. Spread on greased and floured jelly roll pan. Bake at 350-375 degrees for 20-25 minutes. Cool and frost if desired.

Maxine Bowles

COCONUT MACAROONS

2 egg whites
1 teaspoon almond or vanilla
   extract
½ teaspoon salt

1 cup sugar
2 cups coconut, shredded or
   flaked

Line cookie sheet with brown paper. Beat egg whites until stiff. Gradually beat in extract, salt and sugar. Fold in the coconut. Drop on paper lined pan by the teaspoonful. Bake for 15 minutes in a preheated 325 degree oven until golden brown.

Note: These can be frozen and will thaw in 5-10 minutes.

Shirley F. Burd

COCONUT TEACAKES

1 cup sugar
½ cup butter or margarine
1 egg
½ teaspoon vanilla
½ teaspoon baking powder

½ cup coconut, grated or flaked
pinch of salt
½ cup oatmeal (optional)
1½ cups flour

Mix together sugar, butter (or margarine), egg, vanilla, baking powder, coconut, salt and oatmeal (if desired). Add flour and blend well. Drop dough by the teaspoonful on a well greased cookie sheet. Bake in a preheated 350 degree oven for 20 minutes. Makes 2½ to 3 dozen cookies.

Marjean Goodman

COCOONS

1 cup butter
2 cups nuts, chopped
2 cups flour
2 cups sugar

2 teaspoons vanilla
pinch of salt
powdered sugar

Melt butter, stir in nuts, flour, sugar, vanilla and salt. Form into cocoon shapes. Bake on ungreased cookie sheet in a preheated 325 degree oven for 10-12 minutes or until barely browned on bottom. Roll in powdered sugar.

Mary Pat Van Epps

QUICK CRUNCHY COOKIES

1 box honey graham crackers
½ cup butter

½ cup sugar
1 cup pecans, crushed

Lay whole graham crackers flat on a 12x18 inch cookie sheet. Put butter, margarine and sugar in sauce pan and boil 2 minutes (this is a must). Stir occasionally. Sprinkle pecans over graham crackers. Pour sauce over crackers and pecans. Bake in a 350 degree oven for 8 minutes. Cool. Store in covered tin.

Kay Fallin

FRUIT CAKE COOKIES

½ cup brown sugar
¼ cup butter
2 eggs, beaten
1½ cups flour
1 tablespoon milk
½ teaspoon soda
4 tablespoons orange juice
¼ teaspoon cloves
¼ teaspoon nutmeg

¼ teaspoon allspice
½ teaspoon cinnamon
½ pound candied pineapple, chopped
1 pound candied cherries, chopped
1 pound dates, chopped
1 quart pecans, chopped

Preheat oven to 300 degrees. Grease and flour a large cookie sheet. Combine all ingredients and drop by spoonfuls onto cookie sheet (about 2 inches apart). Bake for 25 minutes and cool on racks. Store in airtight containers or wrapped in aluminum foil. Makes about 5 dozen cookies.

Linda White

GINGERSNAPS

¾ cup cooking oil
1 cup sugar
¼ cup dark molasses
1 egg
2 teaspoons baking soda

2 cups flour, sifted
½ teaspoon cloves
½ teaspoon ginger
1 teaspoon cinnamon
½ teaspoon salt

Mix oil, sugar, molasses and egg together, beat well. Sift together soda, flour, cloves, ginger, cinnamon and salt. Mix well. Form into 1 inch balls, roll in granulated sugar. Place on greased cookie sheet. Bake for 6-8 minutes in a preheated 375 degree oven. Makes 4½ to 5 dozen cookies.

Jo Pool

OATMEAL SPICE COOKIES

1 cup granulated sugar
1 cup brown sugar
1 cup butter or margarine
2 eggs
1 teaspoon vanilla
1½ cups flour

1 teaspoon baking soda
½ teaspoon cinnamon
¼ teaspoon cloves
¼ teaspoon nutmeg
3 cups oatmeal

In a large bowl, cream sugars, butter and eggs. Add vanilla. Mix well. Sift flour and soda, add to butter mixture. Stir in spices. Add oatmeal. Stir after each cup. Preheat oven to 375 degrees. Drop dough by teaspoonfuls onto greased cookie sheet, or shape into little circles. Reduce heat to 350 degrees. Bake for 10-12 minutes. Makes approximately 11½ dozen.

Mary Jones

BUTTERSCOTCH OATMEAL COOKIES

1 cup butter or margarine,
  softened
¾ cup sugar
¾ cup brown sugar
2 eggs
2 teaspoons vanilla
1⅓ cups flour
1 teaspoon baking soda

1 teaspoon baking powder
½ teaspoon salt
2 cups oats, uncooked
¾ cup nuts, chopped
1 (6 ounce) package
  butterscotch chips
¾ cup raisins
¼ cup coconut

Cream together butter and sugars. Add eggs and vanilla and blend well. Add flour, soda, baking powder, and salt and mix well. By hand, add oats, nuts, chips, raisins and coconut. Mix well. Drop by teaspoonful on greased cookie sheet. Bake at 375 degrees for 8 to 10 minutes. Remove immediately and cool on racks.

Mary Pat Van Epps

RAISIN-OATMEAL-NUT COOKIES

1 cup all purpose flour
½ teaspoon salt
½ teaspoon baking powder
¼ teaspoon soda
½ cup melted shortening
1 cup light brown sugar

2 eggs
1 teaspoon vanilla
½ cup nuts, chopped
½ cup white raisins
2 cups oats, uncooked

Sift together flour, salt, baking powder, and soda. Combine melted shortening and brown sugar. Add eggs and vanilla. Beat thoroughly. Stir in sifted flour mixture, add nuts, raisins, and oats. Preheat oven to 375 degrees. Drop by rounded teaspoonful onto lightly greased cookie sheet. Bake for 15 minutes. Yields 3 dozen cookies.

Note: These are very nutritious, lightly flavored cookies, especially enjoyed by children of all ages.

Pat Meade

PUMPKIN COOKIES

1 cup shortening
1 cup sugar
1½ cups pumpkin
1 egg
2 cups flour
1 teaspoon soda

1 teaspoon cinnamon
½ teaspoon salt
1 cup butterscotch pieces
1 cup nuts
1 cup raisins

Cream shortening and sugar, add pumpkin and egg. In another bowl, mix flour, soda, cinnamon and salt. Mix the creamed mixture with the dry ingredients. Stir in butterscotch pieces, nuts and raisins. Preheat oven to 375 degrees. Drop by teaspoonfuls on ungreased sheet. Bake 10-12 minutes. Frost while still warm.

Frosting: Pumpkin Cookies
6 tablespoons butter
8 teaspoons milk
¼ to ½ cup brown sugar

1½ to 2 cups powdered sugar
1½ teaspoons vanilla

Heat butter, milk and brown sugar until sugar dissolves. Stir in powdered sugar and vanilla until mixture is thick enough to frost cookies. Cool frosting.

Stephanie McGhee

GRANDMA'S SUGAR COOKIES

2 cups flour, divided
1½ teaspoons baking powder
½ teaspoon salt
½ cup butter

1 cup sugar
1 egg, well beaten
1 teaspoon vanilla
1 tablespoon milk or cream

In a bowl sift together 1½ cups flour, baking powder, and salt. In another bowl cream butter and sugar, gradually adding sugar until light and fluffy. Add egg, vanilla and milk. Add sifted ingredients; gradually add remaining flour until dough is stiff enough to handle. Chill at least 1 hour. Roll to ⅛ inch thickness on lightly floured board and cut out. Bake in 375 degree oven for 10-15 mintues.

Tine Keller

BASIC SPRITZ COOKIES (with variations)

1 cup butter	**2 teaspoons vanilla**
¼ cup margarine	**2¼ cups all purpose flour**
¾ cup granulated sugar	**¼ teaspoon baking powder**
1 large egg	**¼ teaspoon salt**

Cream butter and margarine until soft. Add sugar gradually, cream 5 minutes until light and fluffy. Add egg and vanilla, beat well. Sift flour, baking powder and salt together. Add in 3 additions, mix well after each addition. Shape dough into rolls, wrap in waxed paper, refrigerate for 1 hour. Put through cookie press or drop from spoon onto cookie sheet. Preheat oven to 375 degrees. Bake 7-8 minutes or until edges turn light brown. Makes 6-7 dozen cookies using cookie press.

Variations

Coffee-Maple—Substitute two teaspoons maple extract for vanilla and add 2 teaspoons instant coffee powder.

Lemon Cookies—Substitute 2 teaspoons lemon extract for vanilla. Add 1 tablespoon freshly grated lemon peel.

Eggnog Cookies—Add ½ teaspoon nutmeg to flour mixture.

Raspberry-nut Cookies—Substitute 1½ teaspoons coconut or black walnut extract for vanilla. Add 2 tablespoons seedless red raspberry jam. Sprinkle with chopped nuts before baking.

Chocolate-Almond Cookies—Decrease vanilla to 1 teaspoon. Add 1 teaspoon almond extract and 3 tablespoons cocoa.

Orange Cookies—Substitute 2 teaspoons orange extract for vanilla. Add 1 tablespoon freshly grated orange peel.

Note: If refrigerated longer than one hour, allow to stand at room temperature for 15-30 minutes before putting through cookie press.

Martha C. Yancey

SCOTCH TEAS

½ cup butter
1 cup light brown sugar
2 cups rolled oats

½ teaspoon salt
1 teaspoon baking powder

Preheat oven to 350 degrees. Melt butter and sugar. Stir in rolled oats, salt, and baking powder; mix well. Pour into greased 8x8 inch pan and bake in about 30 minutes. Cool and cut into small squares. Makes 1½ dozen squares.

Leon S. McAulay

GREAT GRANDMA'S TEA CAKES

3 or 4 cups flour
3 cups sugar
3 eggs
1 cup butter
1 cup sour milk

½ teaspoon salt
1 teaspoon soda
1 teaspoon vanilla
1 teaspoon lemon juice

Measure flour into a large pan. In the center of the flour make a hole big enough to hold remaining ingredients. Add them all and knead the dough as if making biscuits. Work until dough is stiff enough to roll out and cut with a cookie cutter. Bake in a 400 degree oven until brown. Makes 3 or 4 dozen.

Myra Tillis

GRANDMA'S TURKISH COOKIES

2 cups powdered sugar
1 cup butter, melted (no substitutions)

1 egg yolk
¾ cup flour

Combine sugar and butter and beat until light and fluffy, about 20 minutes. Add egg yolk and continue beating. Add flour gradually and beat until mixture is elastic, about 20 minutes. Form into balls on ungreased cookie sheet and bake at 275 degrees for 20 minutes. The color remains creamy yellow, and cookies should be dried out, not burned! Yield: 9 dozen.

Tine Keller

BOURBON BALLS

2½ cups vanilla wafers, finely
crushed
1 cup English walnuts, finely
crushed
1 cup powdered sugar

2 tablespoons cocoa
3 tablespoons corn syrup
⅓ cup bourbon
½ cup powdered sugar
1 teaspoon instant coffee

Combine wafers, walnuts, 1 cup sugar, cocoa, syrup and bourbon, mixing well. Using your hands, shape into 1 inch balls. Mix together ½ cup powdered sugar and coffee. Roll each ball in powdered sugar coating. Makes 36 bourbon balls.

Ann Latimer

DIVINITY

2½ cups sugar
½ cup water
½ cup white corn syrup
2 egg whites

1 teaspoon flavoring (vanilla,
rum, orange, etc)
3 or 4 drops food coloring

Cook sugar, water and syrup until if forms a semi-hard ball when dropped in cold water. Beat egg whites at room temperature until stiff, add flavoring and food coloring. Pour hot syrup mixture into egg whites while mixing. Continue to beat until mixture becomes stiff. Spoon out on waxed paper, using teaspoon for generous size piece of candy.

Tom Proctor

"NEVER FAIL" CHOCOLATE -NUT FUDGE

2 cups sugar
2 tablespoons cocoa
½ cup milk
½ cup light corn syrup

1 teaspoon vanilla
½ cup margarine
1 cup nuts, chopped

Stir together sugar, cocoa, milk, and syrup. Boil until it forms a soft ball when dropped into a cup of cold water. Remove from heat and add vanilla and margarine. Let set about 10 minutes to cool, then beat until it begins to harden. Add nuts and pour into a greased 9x9 inch pan. Let cool and cut into squares.

Diana Smith

LUCILLE'S IRON SKILLET PEANUT BRITTLE

2 cups sugar
1 cup light corn syrup
½ cup water
2 cups raw peanuts, shelled

1 tablespoon butter
1 teaspoon vanilla
2 teaspoons soda

Boil sugar, syrup and water in iron skillet to 280 degrees using a candy thermometer. (If you don't have one, heat until a drop of the mixture cracks when dropped into cold water). Add the peanuts and cook 3 more minutes. Remove from burner. Add butter and vanilla and stir well. Then stir in soda and let it foam. Pour onto buttered cookie sheet, let harden, then break into pieces. Yields: " Quite a little bit."

Tine Keller

CHOCOLATE PEANUT BUTTER FUDGE

2 cups sugar
¼ cup light corn syrup
½ cup milk
3 tablespoons cocoa
pinch of salt

6 heaping tablespoons peanut
  butter
1 tablespoon butter
1 tablespoon vanilla

In a sauce pan mix together sugar, corn syrup, milk, cocoa, salt and peanut butter. Place over heat and boil just 4 minutes from the time bubbles form all over the pan. Remove from heat and add butter and vanilla, stirring to melt the butter. Place sauce pan in a pan of cold water and allow to cool until you can hold your hand on the bottom of the pan. Beat fudge until it just begins to thicken. Pour into a 9x9 inch buttered pan. Allow to harden and cut into squares.

Tine Keller

Pies

APPLE PIE

5-7 tart apples
¾ - 1 cup sugar
2 tablespoons flour
dash salt
1 teaspoon cinnamon
¼ teaspoon nutmeg
2 tablespoons butter or
    margarine

1 tablespoon lemon juice or
    grated peel if apples are not
    tart
pie crust, top and bottom,
    unbaked

Pare apples and slice thin. Mix sugar, flour, salt and spices; add to apples and mix. Put in pie shell and dot with butter. Adjust top crust, perforate with knife and dot with butter. Bake for 50 minutes in a preheated 400 degree oven.

Note: If using prepared pie crusts, use one for the bottom crust and mold another to fit the top of the pie.

Margaret Jenkins

DUTCH APPLE PIE

4 large apples
1 (9 inch) pie shell, uncooked
1 cup sugar, divided
1 teaspoon cinnamon
3 tablespoons maraschino
    cherry juice

¾ cup flour
½ cup butter
½ cup pecans, chopped

Peel, slice and arrange apples in pie shell. Sprinkle with ½ cup of the sugar mixed with cinnamon. Add cherry juice. Sift remaining sugar with flour and cut in butter until crumbly. Add nuts and crumble evenly over apples. Bake until tender (about 1 hour) in a preheated 350 degree oven.

Kitty Cashion

NOT SO RICH BANANA CREAM PIE

⅓ cup non fat dry milk solids
⅓ cup sugar
3 tablespoons corn starch
⅛ teaspoon salt
1⅔ cup water

3 egg yolks
1 teaspoon vanilla
1½ cups sliced ripe bananas
3 egg whites
6 tablespoons sugar

Mix dry milk, sugar corn starch, salt, water and egg yolks in blender. Blend for ½ to 1 minute. Cook in 1½ quart sauce pan over medium heat, stirring constantly until thick and smooth, about 5 minutes. Stir in vanilla. Cover and cool thoroughly. Pour half of cooled custard into a cold baked 9 inch pie shell. Spread sliced bananas evenly over custard. Cover with remaining custard. Preheat oven to 350 degrees. Beat 3 egg whites and 6 table-spoons sugar until stiff. Spread over custard, spreading to edge of crust to seal in filling. Bake for 15 minutes or until meringue is light brown.

Pat Meade

BLUEBERRY CREAM CHEESE TORTS

Nut Crust
½ cup margarine, softened
¼ cup brown sugar

1 cup all purpose flour
½ cup nuts, chopped

Preheat oven to 375 degrees. Blend all ingredients and pat out in bottom of 9x13 inch pan. Bake for 15 minutes. (Do not allow to brown.) Remove from oven and crumble with spoon at once and spread evenly in bottom of pan.

Filling
1 (8 ounce) package cream
 cheese, softened to room
 temperature
1 cup powdered sugar
2½ teaspoons milk

1 teaspoon vanilla
2 (1½ ounce) packages Dream
 Whip
1 (22 ounce) can blueberry pie
 filling

Combine cheese, sugar, milk and vanilla and blend well. Prepare 2 pack-ages of Dream Whip according to directions. Fold into the cheese mixture. Spread on crust. Top with 1 can blueberry pie filling. Chill, cut into squares. Serves 15-16.

Betty Jo Walker

CANNED FRUIT COBBLER

½ cup butter or margarine
1 cup granulated sugar
¾ cup flour
2 teaspoons baking powder

⅛ teaspoon salt
¾ cup milk
1 (16 ounce) can fruit (peach, cherry, or blueberry)

Preheat oven to 350 degrees. Melt butter or margarine in a deep baking dish. Make batter of sugar, flour, baking powder, salt and milk. Pour over melted butter. Do not stir! Pour fruit, including syrup, on top of batter. Do not stir! Bake 1 hour.

Pat Meade

EASY FRUIT COBBLER

¼ cup butter
1 quart cooked sweetened fruit
1 cup flour

1 cup sugar
3 teaspoons baking powder
1 cup milk

Preheat oven to 375 degrees. Melt butter in a 9x9 inch baking dish. Heat fruit in a saucepan. Mix together flour, sugar, baking powder and milk. This batter will be thin. Pour batter into buttered dish. Add heated fruit to top of batter. Bake 30 minutes and serve warm.

Linda White

VANILLA CREAM PIE WITH VARIATIONS

¾ cup sugar
2 tablespoons flour
3 tablespoons cornstarch
¼ teaspoon salt
2 cups milk

2 eggs, separated
1 tablespoon butter
2 teaspoons vanilla
baked or crumb pie crust

Mix sugar, flour, cornstarch and salt in top of double boiler. Add milk slowly. Stir and cook until boiling point is reached. Cook for 20 minutes, stirring occasionally. Add well beaten egg yolks and butter and stir for 2 minutes. Remove from heat and add vanilla and fruits or flavors. (See variations below.) Pour into crumb or baked pastry crust. Top with meringue and brown in oven.

Variations

Pineapple—add 1 cup drained crushed pineapple just before removing from heat.

Bananas—add 2 sliced bananas.

Coconut —add 1 cup shredded coconut.

Chocolate—3 tablespoons cocoa mixing cocoa with flour.

Note: Cornstarch may be omitted if flour is increased to 7 tablespoons

Margaret Jenkins

CHOCOLATE CHIP PIE

½ cup butter, softened
1 cup sugar
1 teaspoon chocolate flavoring
4 eggs
1 cup white corn syrup

6 ounces semisweet chocolate chips
1 cup pecans, chopped
1 (9 inch) "deep dish" pie crust, unbaked

Preheat oven to 350 degrees. Cream butter and sugar. Blend in the vanilla, eggs and syrup. Add chocolate chips and nuts. Turn into unbaked pie crust and bake for 50-55 minutes. Cool before serving. Serves 6 to 8.

Lynne Gorline

FRENCH SILK CHOCOLATE PIE

½ cup butter or margarine
¾ cup sugar
2 squares unsweetened
    chocolate, melted

1 teaspoon vanilla
2 eggs
1 baked pie crust
Whipped cream

Cream butter and sugar until creamy. Add melted chocolate, vanilla and one egg. Beat for 3 minutes. Add the other egg and beat 3 minutes more. Pour into baked crust, chill. Top with whipped cream.

Marcia Armstrong

CHOCOLATE DELIGHT

Graham Cracker Crust
½ cup margarine
1 cup flour

1 cup graham crackers, crushed
1 cup pecans, chopped

Chocolate Filling
8 ounces cream cheese,
  softened
1 cup powdered sugar
2 (8 ounce) cartons Cool Whip
1 (3¾ ounces) package vanilla
  pudding

1 (3¾ ounce) package
  chocolate pudding
3 cups sweet milk

Preheat oven to 350 degrees. Combine margarine, flour, graham crackers crumbs and pecans in 9x13 inch pan. Press mixture into bottom of pan. Bake 10 minutes at 350 degrees. Cool. Combine softened cream cheese, powdered sugar and one (8 ounce) carton Cool Whip. Beat well with mixer. Spread this layer over crust. Run knife under hot water to ease spreading. Mix vanilla and chocolate pudding mixes with milk and allow to set for several minutes. Pour pudding mixture over cream cheese layer. Top with remaining carton of Cool Whip. Chill.

Peggy Sparrenberger

SCRUMPTIOUS PIE

LAYER 1 (Crust)
½ cup butter, softened
1 cup flour

1 tablespoon sugar
½ cup nuts, chopped

LAYER 2
1 (8 ounce) package cream
  cheese

1 cup powdered sugar
2 cups Cool Whip

LAYER 3
2 (6 ounce) boxes, instant
  chocolate pudding
2 (6 ounce) boxes, instant
  vanilla pudding

6 cups milk

LAYER 4
2 cups Cool Whip

Preheat oven to 350 degrees. Mix the softened butter, flour, sugar and nuts for a pie crust. Press in 9x13 inch pan and bake 15 minutes; cool. Cream together cream cheese and the powdered sugar. Fold in the Cool Whip and pour on cooled crust. Mix together the dry chocolate and vanilla puddings. Add 6 cups milk and mix until thick. Pour on top of previous layer. Top with Cool Whip and chill.

Debbie McCanless

FUDGE PIE

1 cup butter or margarine
½ cup flour
½ cup cocoa

2 cups sugar
4 eggs, separated
1 teaspoon vanilla

Melt butter in saucepan. Stir in flour, cocoa, sugar, egg yolks and vanilla. Preheat oven to 375 degrees. Beat egg whites until stiff and fold into fudge mixture. Pour into a 9 or 10 inch greased pie pan and bake for 15 minutes. Reduce heat to 350 degrees and bake 30 minutes longer. May be served warm with whipped cream or ice cream.

June Ward

YUMMY FUDGE PIE

3 tablespoons cocoa
1 cup sugar
¼ cup flour
pinch of salt

2 large eggs, beaten
1 teaspoon vanilla
¼ cup butter, melted
½ cup nuts, chopped

Preheat oven to 350 degrees. Mix all ingredients together and pour into a greased and floured 8 or 9 inch pie pan. Bake for 20-25 minutes.

Libby Parker

COCONUT PIE

4 eggs
1 cup sugar
2 cups milk
½ cup margarine

½ cup flour
1 teaspoon vanilla
1 cup coconut
Nutmeg or cinnamon, to taste

Preheat oven to 350 degrees. Place all ingredients into blender and beat until smooth. Pour into greased 9 inch glass pie plate. Bake 1 hour or until set. Sprinkle top with nutmeg or cinnamon. Serves 8.

Margaret Jenkins

NOT SO RICH LEMON MERINGUE PIE

⅓ cup non-fat dry milk solids
1 cup sugar
¼ cup corn starch
¼ teaspoon salt
3 egg yolks

1⅔ cup water
½ cup lemon juice
9 or 10 inch baked pastry shell
3 egg whites
6 tablespoons sugar

Mix dry milk, sugar, corn starch and salt in 1½ quart saucepan. Add egg yolks and water, stir or mix well with electric mixer. (This can be run through blender to save time). Cook and stir over medium heat 6 minutes or until thick. Then, cook over low heat 5 minutes longer. Remove from heat. Stir in lemon juice. Cool thoroughly. Pour into cold cooked pastry shell. Preheat oven to 350 degrees. Top with meringue made with 3 egg whites and 6 tablespoons sugar beaten until stiff. Bake for 15 minutes or until light brown. Cut with wet knife after thoroughly cooked.

Pat Meade

GRANDMA'S BEST PECAN PIE

1 9 inch pie pastry, unbaked
¾ cup sugar
1 cup dark corn syrup
3 eggs, slightly beaten

4 tablespoons butter
1 teaspoon vanilla
1 cup pecans, coarsely broken

Preheat oven to 350 degrees. Line 9 inch pie plate with pastry. Boil sugar and syrup together for 2 minutes. Pour slowly over beaten eggs stirring vigorously. Add butter, vanilla and pecans. Pour into unbaked pastry shell. Bake for 50-60 minutes.

Tine Keller

ROYAL LIME CHIFFON PIE

1 tablespoon cornstarch	3 egg whites
1½ cups cold water	¼ cup sugar
1 (3¾ ounce) package lime gelatin	1 baked pie shell

Combine cornstarch and cold water in sauce pan. Bring mixture to boil. Remove from heat and stir in lime gelatin. Continue stirring until gelatin is dissolved. Chill until slightly thickened. Beat egg whites, gradually adding sugar. Beat until stiff and dry. Fold into thickened gelatin mixture. Pile into pie shell. Chill until firm.

Carolyn M. Oxford

PIÑA COLADA PIE

1 (14 ounce) can sweetened condensed milk	3 teaspoons rum flavoring or rum
1 (15¼ ounce) can crushed pineapple, drained	1 (8 ounce) can coconut milk
1 (8 ounce) carton Cool Whip	1 prepared graham cracker pie crust

Mix milk, pineapple, Cool Whip, rum flavoring and coconut milk together. Pour into graham cracker crust. Place pie in freezer. Remove from freezer 10 minutes before serving.

Helen Smith

KENTUCKY PECAN PIE

1 cup white corn syrup	3 whole eggs, slightly beaten
1 cup dark brown sugar	1 9 inch pie pastry, unbaked
⅓ cup butter, melted	1 heaping cup pecan nut meats
⅓ teaspoon salt	1 cup whipping cream, whipped
1 teaspoon vanilla	and sweetened

Preheat oven to 350 degrees. Combine syrup, sugar, butter, salt and vanilla and mix well. Add beaten eggs and stir well. Pour into a 9 inch unbaked pie shell. Sprinkle pecans over all. Bake 45 minutes. Cool and top with whipped cream when ready to serve.

Marie Campbell

PECAN PIE

1 cup white corn syrup
1 cup light brown sugar
⅓ cup butter, melted
3 eggs

1 heaping cup pecans
1 teaspoon vanilla
dash of salt
1 unbaked pie shell (9 inch)

Preheat oven to 350 degrees. Mix all ingredients in large bowl with spoon. Pour into unbaked pie shell. Bake for 45-50 minutes.

Bonnie Williams

OLD FASHIONED PUMPKIN PIE

2 eggs, slightly beaten
2 cups canned or cooked
   pumpkin
¾ cup granulated sugar
½ teaspoon salt
1 teaspoon ground cinnamon

½ teaspoon ground ginger
¼ teaspoon ground cloves
1⅔ cup evaporated milk, top
   milk or milk
1 9 inch unbaked pastry shell

Preheat oven to 425 degrees. Mix ingredients in order given. Pour into pastry shell. Bake for 15 minutes. Reduce heat to 350 degrees and continue baking for 45 minutes or until knife inserted into center comes out clean.

Note: Cooked squash may be substituted for pumpkin. Fresh pumpkin or squash should be steamed with very little or no water as it makes its own juice.

Pat Meade

CREAM CHEESE PASTRY

1 (10 ounce) package pie crust
   mix
1 (3 ounce) package cream
   cheese

1 tablespoon milk

Preheat oven to 400 degrees. Blend ingredients together. Divide dough in half and roll out on floured pastry board. Fit into 9 inch pie pans and bake until lightly browned (approximately 10 minutes). Cool and fill with your favorite filling. Makes 2 crusts.

Martha C. Yancey

Miscellaneous
Desserts

QUICK BANANA PUDDING

2 (3¾ ounce) boxes instant
vanilla pudding
1 (3¾ ounce) box instant
coconut pudding

1 (9-10 ounce) carton Cool Whip
or other whipped topping
1 box vanilla wafers
bananas, sliced

Prepare pudding mixes according to package directions, using low fat milk. Stir puddings together and fold in whipped topping. Line a casserole dish with vanilla wafers. Place a layer of sliced bananas over the wafers and spread with a layer of pudding. Continue layers of wafers, bananas and pudding until all of pudding is used. Top layer should be pudding.

Ruth R. Quin

BERRY PUDDING

1 quart berries (black
raspberries or blackberries)
1 (18½ ounce) package white
cake mix, or 1 egg cake.

flour
Hard Sauce
cream or milk (optional)

Drain the canned berries, or clean and drain fresh berries. Prepare batter for the white cake mix or the 1 egg cake according to directions. Roll the berries in flour; fold into the cake batter. Pour the batter into a greased and floured 9x13 inch pan. Bake according to cake directions. Check with a straw as 10 to 15 more minutes may be necessary. Serve hot with cream or milk if you can depart from your diet in a big way!

Hard Sauce
½ cup butter or margarine
1 (1 pound) box powdered
sugar

1 tablespoon vanilla or brandy

Place butter in bowl and allow to soften well at room temperature. Work sugar and vanilla into the butter. Pack into a bowl and chill. Score or cut into serving pieces. Serve on *hot* berry pudding, steamed puddings, mincemeat pie or apple pie.

Shirley F. Burd

CREAM PUFFS WITH FILLING

1 cup water, boiling
1½ cups butter or margarine
⅛ teaspoon salt
1 cup flour, sifted

4 eggs
whipped cream, sweetened
strawberry slices
powdered sugar

Combine water, butter and salt in a saucepan, bring to a boil. Add flour and stir vigorously until mixture forms a ball and leaves sides of pan. Remove from heat. Add eggs, one at a time, beating thoroughly after each one. Continue beating until dough is stiff. Drop by the tablespoonful on a well greased cookie sheet, 3 or 4 inches apart. Bake in 450 degree oven for 20 minutes. Reduce heat to 350 degrees and continue baking until firm and golden. Cool on rack. Cut off tops and fill with whipped cream and strawberries. Replace tops and sprinkle with powdered sugar. Yield 10-12 puffs.

Note: These are very easy to make.

Variation: You may substitute any flavor of pudding for the whipped cream and strawberries. Be sure the pudding is cooled before using.

Pat Meade

BAKED CUSTARD

⅓ cup sugar
½ teaspoon salt
1 teaspoon vanilla

4 eggs, slightly beaten
3 cups milk, scalded
nutmeg

Add sugar, salt and vanilla to beaten eggs. Gradually add scalded milk, stirring constantly. Pour into custard cups or casserole dish. Sprinkle with nutmeg and place in pan containing hot water. Water level should be to level of custard in cups. Bake at 375 degrees for 30 minutes or until a knife inserted in center comes out clean.

Mary Pat Van Epps

FUDGE SAUCE

¼ cup butter or margarine
2 squares bitter chocolate
⅛ teaspoon salt
1½ cups sugar

1 cup, less 2 tablespoons,
  evaporated milk
1 teaspoon vanilla

Heat butter and chocolate in top of double boiler over simmering water until melted. Stir in salt and sugar in 4 or 5 portions, being sure to blend sugar thoroughly after each addition. The mixture will be thick and grainy. Stir in milk slowly. Cook 5-6 minutes until smooth and thickened, stirring frequently. Remove from heat. Stir in vanilla. Pour into glass jar with tight fitting lid, cover and cool, then store in refrigerator. To heat, set jar in warm water 30 minutes before use. Change water once or twice as necessary. Store unused portion in refrigerator. Keeps well. Makes 1 pint.

Mary Gowan

CHOCOLATE FLAVORED SYRUP (LOW CALORIE)

⅓ cup powdered cocoa
1¼ cups cold water
¼ teaspoon salt

2 teaspoons vanilla
sweetener to substitute for
  ½ cup sugar

Combine cocoa, water and salt in a heavy saucepan. Mix until smooth. Bring to a boil and simmer stirring constantly until thick and smooth. Remove from heat and allow to cool for 10 minutes. Add vanilla and artificial sweetener. Mix well. Pour into a jar with tight fitting lid and store in refrigerator. Stir well before each use. 1 tablespoon: 9 calories.

Carolyn Foster

LOW CALORIE GELATIN

1 (1 tablespoon) package
  unflavored gelatin
½ cup water
artificial sweetener for ½ cup
  beverage

1 (12 ounce) can sugarfree,
  flavored soft drink

Sprinkle gelatin over water. Heat in sauce pan until gelatin dissolves. Add sweetener and stir. Stir in soft drink. Pour into dessert dishes and chill until firm.

Carolyn Foster

BOURBON ICE CREAM

½ gallon of the best vanilla ice
cream
2 dozen bakery-made coconut
macaroons

1 cup bourbon

Let ice cream soften slightly. Crumble macaroons. Put all ingredients in a large chilled bowl, mix well and return to freezer.

June Ward

CHOCOLATE ICE CREAM

2 squares unsweetened
chocolate
1 (14 ounce) can sweetened
condensed milk

2 cups light cream
1 cup cold water
1 teaspoon vanilla

Heat chocolate and milk in a double boiler, stirring frequently until chocolate is melted and thickened. Combine cream, water and vanilla with chocolate mixture and chill. Freeze in ice cream freezer.

Margaret Jenkins

COCONUT ICE CREAM

6 eggs
1⅓ cups sugar
2 (14 ounce) cans sweetened
condensed milk

½ gallon whole milk
½ teaspoon coconut flavoring
1 cup coconut, grated

Beat eggs and sugar well. Add condensed milk, whole milk, coconut flavoring and grated coconut; mix well. Freeze in ice cream freezer.

Margaret Jenkins

CREAMY VANILLA ICE CREAM

5 eggs	pinch salt
2 tablespoons vanilla	5½ cups homogenized milk
1¾ cups sugar	1 quart half and half

Beat eggs well. Combine with all other ingredients and place in a 5 quart ice cream freezer. Freeze according to freezer instructions. Yields 5 quarts.

Peggy Tagg

VANILLA ICE CREAM

13 cups homogenized milk	1 tablespoon vanilla
pinch salt	4-5 eggs
1½ cups sugar	

Fill up ice cream freezer with milk. Add salt. Mix sugar, vanilla, and eggs well. Add to milk mixture. Freeze according to freezer instructions.

Note: For variety, add two cups crushed fruit with milk.
Yields 5 quarts.

Peggy Tagg

VANILLA ICE CREAM WITH A TOUCH OF. . .

1 quart vanilla ice cream, softened	3 teaspoons Creme de Menthe
⅓ cup pecans, chopped	
⅓ cup preserved ginger, chopped - (available at Chinese Food Store)	

Mix ingredients together and refreeze stirring occasionally to distribute additions evenly.

Grace M. Wallace

LEMON SNOW WITH GRAND MARNIER SAUCE

1 envelope gelatin, unflavored
⅔ cup sugar
1½ cups water, boiling
¼-½ teaspoon lemon peel,
   finely grated

⅓ cup lemon juice (fresh)
3 egg whites

In large bowl mix gelatin and sugar. Add boiling water and stir until gelatin dissolves. Add lemon peel and juice. Chill until syrupy. (½ hour in ice bath or 1 hour in refrigerator). Beat egg whites until stiff. Add to lemon mixture and beat until it begins to thicken slightly, about 5 minutes. Pour into serving dish and chill until set - at least 2 hours.

Grand Marnier Sauce
½ cup heavy cream
3 egg yolks
¼ cup sugar
⅓ cup butter, very soft
3 tablespoons lemon juice,
   fresh

3 tablespoons Grand Marnier
1 teaspoon lemon peel, finely
   grated

Pour cream into bowl and set in ice bath. Beat cream till thick and glossy but not stiff. Refrigerate. Beat egg yolks until thick and lemon colored, gradually adding sugar. Slowly beat in butter, lemon juice and liqueur. Fold in lemon peel and whipped cream. Chill. Ladle sauce over lemon snow as served.

Pat Hickman

ORANGE FLUFF

2 (6 ounce) packages orange
   gelatin

1 (4 ounce) carton Cool Whip,
   divided

Follow directions on package for mixing gelatin. Pour into an 18x18 inch pan, and chill until slightly thickened. Fold 2 ounces of the Cool Whip into chilled gelatin. Chill for 30 minutes. Top with remaining 2 ounces of Cool Whip. Makes 12 (½ cup) servings.

Note: For diet user: Substitute low calorie orange gelatin
Substitute non-calorie Whipped Topping for topping

Margaret Toler

BAKED CRISPY PEACHES

1 (20 ounce) can peach halves
1 cup corn flakes
3 tablespoons brown sugar

1 tablespoon butter or
margarine

Drain peach halves, reserving juice. Crush corn flakes. Lightly roll peach halves in cornflakes. Place peaches, hollow side up, in baking dish. Fill centers with brown sugar. Dot with butter or margarine. Pour juice around peaches. Bake at 375 degrees for about 25 minutes or until browned. Serve warm with cream or evaporated milk.

Catherine Pfeiffer

MOMMA'S PEACH FREEZE

1 (29 ounce) can cling peaches,
  drained
1 (16 ounce) can cling peaches,
  drained
⅓ cup fresh lemon juice

1 teaspoon lemon rind, grated
⅔ cup granulated sugar
1 tablespoon cold water
1 teaspoon unflavored gelatin

Put all ingredients in blender and blend well. Pour into a 2 quart dish and freeze. Let stand at room temperature 15 minutes before serving. Makes 6-8 servings.

Patricia D. Hallmark

ORANGE SHERBET

6 (6 ounce) bottles orange drink
1 (14 ounce) can sweetened
  condensed milk
1 (8 ounce) can crushed
  pineapple

1 cup maraschino cherries,
  chopped

Pour all ingredients into ice cream freezer. Add ice and ice cream salt according to freezer instructions. Freeze according to freezer instructions (hand freezer: crank will be very difficult to turn). Let sit for 30 minutes. Makes 1 gallon.

Jo Pool

PINK DELIGHT DESSERT

1 (22 ounce) can cherry pie
  filling
1 (16 ounce) can crushed
  pineapple, drained

1 (10 ounce) can sweetened
  condensed milk
1 (12 ounce) carton Cool Whip

Mix all ingredients together. Chill 2 hours or longer in refrigerator before serving.

Karen Patterson

PISTACHIO CREAM DESSERT

1 (8 ounce) can crushed
  pineapple
1 (3¾ ounce) package instant
  pistachio pudding
1 cup miniature marshmallows,
  cut up

1 (8 ounce) carton Cool Whip
1 (5 ounce) package pistachio
  nuts, chopped

Combine undrained pineapple with the dry pudding mix in a large bowl. Blend in marshmallows, Cool Whip and nuts. Mix well. Chill in refrigerator before serving.

Betty Gray

RICE PUDDING

4 tablespoons rice, uncooked
3 tablespoons sugar
1 quart milk
½ teaspoon salt

½ cup seedless raisins
1 teaspoon vanilla
½ teaspoon nutmeg

Combine rice, sugar, milk and salt in a (1½ quart) baking dish. Bake at 350 degrees for two hours until rice is very well done. Stir several times while baking. Stir in the raisins and vanilla. Sprinkle with the nutmeg and continue baking until a light brown crust forms, about 20 minutes. Serve either warm or cold. 5-6 servings.

Note: Don't substitute other types of rice for the regular rice. This is a creamy pudding, *not* one that can be "cut!"

Katherine Horton Farley

ENGLISH SHERRY TRIFLE

There are as many ways of making trifle as there are people who make it. This is mine — it's tried and true and is well liked by my friends.

1 (16 ounce) pound cake (preferably stale)
1 (17 ounce) can fruit cocktail
1 cup sherry
2 cups vanilla custard sauce (see below)

1 cup heavy cream
½ tablespoon sugar
Decorations, e.g. glacé cherries, split blanched almonds, nonpareils, whatever is on hand.

Slice cake in ½ inch slices the night before. Leave exposed to the air on a tray or plate overnight so that the cake will dry out.

Line a glass dish or bowl (your prettiest and best!) with half of the slices of cake. Drain the fruit cocktail and reserve the syrup. Arrange half of the fruit over the cake. Add another layer of cake and top it with the remaining fruit. Pour the sherry over the contents of the bowl, tipping the bowl from side to side to ensure that the cake is well soaked with sherry. Make the custard sauce (below). While hot, pour the sauce over the cake and fruit to cover. Set aside to cool and set. When cool, whip heavy cream with sugar and pile over the cool custard. Decorate to your fancy.

Note: If your guests will include children or adults who don't use alcohol, a second bowl of trifle can be made using the reserved syrup to soak the cake instead of the sherry. Be sure to mark which is which!

Vanilla Custard Sauce
This stands up better than an egg custard sauce!
2 cups milk
2 level tablespoons cornstarch
1 tablespoon sugar

1 teaspoon vanilla
yellow food coloring
¼ cup butter, cut into bits

Place milk in a sauce pan over moderate heat. In a bowl, mix cornstarch and sugar into a smooth paste using a little of the milk. Gradually add the remaining warm milk, mix well and return it to the pan. Bring to a simmer, stirring continously with a wooden spoon until mixture thickens enough to coat the spoon. Remove from the heat Add vanilla. Add food coloring, a drop at a time stirring to mix well until a *pale* yellow color. Beat in butter until melted and absorbed. Pour immediately on the trifle.

Brenda Coulehan

STRAWBERRY BANANA SUPREME

2 cups water, boiling
1 (6 ounce) package strawberry
  gelatin
1 cup water, cold
1½ cups frozen or fresh
  strawberries

1 cup bananas, sliced
1 (8 ounce) can crushed
  pineapple

Filling:
1 (8 ounce) carton sour cream
  (1 cup)

⅓ cup powdered sugar
½ cup pecans, chopped

Topping
1 (8 ounce) carton Cool Whip

Add the boiling water to gelatin and stir until dissolved. Add the cold water and stir. Add strawberries, bananas, and pineapple. Pour half of this mixture into a 7x11 inch glass dish. Place in freezer until mixture is set. Keep the other half at room temperature so it will not congeal. Blend sour cream, powdered sugar, and nuts together. Spread half of this over congealed mixture, then pour remaining gelatin mixture over this; chill until congealed. Spread remaining half of sour cream mixture over this. Top with Cool Whip and chill. Serves 8.

Lila Zaricor

FROSTY STRAWBERRY SQUARES

1 cup flour, sifted
¼ cup brown sugar
½ cup pecans, chopped
½ cup butter, melted
2 egg whites
1 cup sugar

2 cups fresh strawberries,
  sliced or (10 ounce) package
  frozen strawberries
2 teaspoons lemon juice
1 cup Dream Whip or Cool Whip

Heat oven to 350 degrees. Stir together the flour, sugar, pecans and butter. Spread evenly in shallow baking pan. Bake 20 minutes, stirring occasionally. Sprinkle two-thirds of this crumbled mixture in 13x9x2 inch baking pan. Combine egg whites, sugar, berries and lemon juice in large bowl. Beat at high speed until stiff peaks form (about 10 minutes). Fold in Dream Whip. Spoon over crumb mixture in baking pan, and top with remaining crumb mixture. Freeze 6 hours. Cut into squares.

Mary L. Morris

Accompaniments

CITRUS MARMALADE

1 orange
1 grapefruit
1 lemon
⅛ teaspoon baking soda

1½ cups water
5 cups sugar
1 pouch fruit pectin
paraffin

Prepare the fruit by the following: Peel the fruit, taking peel off in quarters or eights. With a vegetable peeler, shave off the rind, discarding at least half of the white portion. Cut this peel up with scissors or sharp knife. Reserve fruit. Add baking soda and water to the chopped peel. Bring to a boil and simmer, covered for 20 minutes. Meanwhile, chop the fruit discarding the fibrous sections and seeds. Add the fruit pulp to the rind mixture and simmer for 10 minutes. Measure 3 cups into a *large* pan or dutch oven. Add sugar and bring to a *rolling* boil. Boil for 1 minute, stirring constantly. Remove from heat and add the fruit pectin. Stir and skim off the foam for 5-10 minutes to prevent fruit from floating on the top. Ladle into glasses and cover with ⅛ inch of hot paraffin.

Note: For gifts, wrap in yellow cellophane and a pretty tie.

Shirley F. Burd

FIG STRAWBERRY PRESERVES

3 cups mashed figs (about 20)
1 (6 ounce) package strawberry
   gelatin

3 cups sugar
paraffin

Thoroughly mix ingredients in large saucepan. Brink to a boil over medium heat and boil 3 minutes, stirring occasionally. Pour quickly into clean glasses. Cover with hot paraffin.

Margaret Jenkins

PEPPER JELLY

¾ cup bell pepper, ground
  (about 5)
½ cup hot pepper, ground
  (about 8-10)
1½ cups apple cider vinegar

6½ cups sugar
large pinch of salt
1 bottle fruit pectin or 2
  pouches
paraffin

Place peppers, vinegar, sugar and salt in a saucepan and boil for 10 minutes, stirring constantly. Skim any residue off the top. Add fruit pectin and stir well. Pour into sterilized jars and seal with paraffin.

Margaret Jenkins

STRAWBERRY JAM

2 quarts ripe strawberries
7 cups sugar
¼ cup lemon juice

½ bottle of fruit pectin, or one
  pouch
paraffin

Mix strawberries, sugar, and lemon juice in a *large* pan or dutch oven. Bring to a rolling boil and boil hard for one minute., stirring constantly. Remove from heat and stir in fruit pectin. Skim off foam with a metal spoon. Stir and skim for ten minutes. Ladle into large or small wine glasses. Cover immediately with ⅛ inch hot paraffin. When cool, wrap with red cellophane and tie at the top for gifts.

Note: Reducing the stirring and skimming time to five minutes is possible, if the fruit is crushed at the beginning. I freeze the berries in their season and make the jam when needed for gifts.

Shirley F. Burd

AU GRATIN CHEESE SAUCE

2 tablespoons butter
2 tablespoons flour
1 teaspoon salt

1 cup milk
1 cup cheese, grated

Melt butter in saucepan. Blend in flour and salt. Gradually add milk and cook until thickened. Add cheese and stir until melted. Can be served with potato or vegetable dishes.

Cindy Hinds

BARBEQUE SAUCE

1 cup ketchup
1 cup water
¼ cup lemon juice
½ cup onion, chopped
5 teaspoons cider vinegar

5 tablespoons brown sugar
5 teaspoons butter
5 tablespoons Worchestershire
    sauce

Boil all ingredients in saucepan for 1 hour over medium heat. Store in tightly closed jar in pantry. To use, pour over cooked pork or beef ribs. Preheat oven to 350 degrees. Bake until sauce bubbles, about 30-45 minutes.

The Committee

DADDY'S COUNTRY BARBEQUE SAUCE

1½ cups vinegar
2 teaspoons salt
1 teaspoon Worcestershire
    sauce
1 teaspoon red pepper sauce

1 tablespoon onion, minced
1 teaspoon garlic powder
¾ cup lemon juice
4 tablespoons butter
1 teaspoon pepper

Place all ingredients in saucepan. Bring to a hard boil (foaming) and boil for 2 minutes. Excellent for grill cooking. Makes enough basting sauce for 1 cut-up chicken or 8 pork chops. Baste frequently.

Tine Keller

ETHEL'S HOMEMADE BARBEQUE SAUCE

1 medium onion, peeled and
chopped
2 tablespoons butter or
margarine
2 tablespoons cider vinegar
2 tablespoons light brown
sugar

4 tablespoons lemon juice
1 cup ketchup
3 tablespoons Worcestershire
sauce
½ cup water
dash salt
dash red pepper

Sauté onions in butter until clear. Add all other ingredients and simmer 10 minutes. Use to baste charcoal-broiled chicken or pork steaks. To use as the sauce for chopped pork or beef barbeque, simmer meat in sauce 1 hour after cooking meat thoroughly.

Patricia D. Hallmark

LOW-CALORIE BARBEQUE SAUCE

4 ounces diet margarine
4 tablespoons Worcestershire
sauce
½ teaspoon cayenne pepper
1 teaspoon hot pepper sauce
⅔ cup cider vinegar

⅔ cup ketchup
2 teaspoons brown sugar
substitute
1 teaspoon onion juice
1 teaspoon salt
¼ teaspoon powdered garlic

Melt margarine and stir in other ingredients. Bring to a boil and stir until well mixed. Ready to use. Recipe may be stored in an air-tight jar in refrigerator.

Pat Meade

HAM SAUCE

1 (10 ounce) can tomato soup,
undiluted
¾ cup vegetable oil
1 cup sugar

¾ cup vinegar
¾ cup prepared mustard
4 egg yolks, slightly beaten

Heat all ingredients in double boiler until mixture thickens. Excellent with ham sandwiches. Can be frozen.

Jane Robilio

BASIC SAUCE OR GRAVY

Thin Sauce
1 tablespoon fat   1 cup fluid
1 tablespoon flour

Medium Sauce
2 tablespoons fat   1 cup fluid
2 tablespoons flour

Thick Sauce
3 tablespoons fat   1 cup fluid
3 tablespoons flour

In a sauce pan or skillet, heat fat until all the water is evaporated. Add flour and cook until light brown and "grainy" feeling against the spoon. Stir frequently. Add fluid, stirring constantly. Cook until sauce thickens and comes to a boil. Remove from heat immediately. If sauce should lump, pour it through a tea strainer and finish cooking in another pot. Next time, make sure all the water is cooked from the fat and that flour is brown.

Note: Fat may be butter, margarine, meat drippings or shortening. Fluid may be milk, meat or fish stock, vegetable or fruit juice.

VARIATIONS FOR BASIC SAUCE

White Sauce: Use butter for the fat and milk for the fluid and prepare in medium sauce proportions. Serve over such things as asparagus or croquettes.

Brown Gravy: Use beef drippings for fat and beef stock or bouillon for the fluid, in the thin or medium proportions. Brown the flour to a very dark color.

Quick Chicken Gravy: Use chicken fat or butter for the fat and a chicken bouillon cube in water for the fluid. Add the crumbs from fried chicken and prepare in medium proportions.

Martha C. Yancey

BERNAISE SAUCE

1 cup butter (no substitute),
   divided
4 egg yolks
3-4 shakes cayenne pepper
salt to taste
1½ tablespoons lemon juice

1 teaspoon tarragon vinegar
1 ounce white wine (or more)
3-4 slices onion, minced
2 cloves garlic, minced
parsley flakes

Melt ½ cup butter. In mixer, beat egg yolks until they are thickened. Add cayenne pepper and salt. Add melted butter VERY SLOWLY. Continue beating. Melt ½ cup butter and add lemon juice. Add this VERY SLOWLY to egg and butter mixture. Add vinegar and continue beating until very thick. Add white wine and beat. Remove from mixer and add minced onion, garlic and parsley flakes. Serve at room temperature or warmed. Excellent with steaks.

Marion Bendersky

PICKLED OKRA

4 pounds small, tender okra
   (with short stems)
10 pods hot pepper, green or
   red
10 cloves garlic

8 cups vinegar
¾ cup salt
1 cup water
celery seed or mustard seed
   (optional)

Wash okra and pack in hot clean pint jars. Place 1 pepper and 1 clove of garlic in each jar. Heat vinegar, salt and water to boiling. Add celery or mustard seed, if desired. Pour hot mixture over okra and seal. Let stand 8 weeks before using. Makes 10 pints.

Margaret Jenkins

SWEET PICKLES

½ gallon medium cucumbers
½ cup plain salt
½ gallon boiling water
¾ ounce alum
1 quart distilled vinegar

¼ to ½ (1¼ ounce) can pickling
  spices
4 pounds sugar
½ gallon boiling water

Wash cucumbers in stone crock. Dissolve salt in ½ gallon boiling water. Pour over cucumbers and let stand 24 hours. Drain. Boil ½ gallon water with alum added and pour over cucumbers. Let stand 24 hours. Drain. Boil the vinegar with the pickling spices. Pour over cucumbers and let stand 8 days. Drain and rinse cucumbers, if desired. Slice cucumbers. Alternate layers of sliced cucumbers and sugar. Cover lightly with cheese cloth. Store for one week, then refrigerate and eat.

Armantine Keller

HOT TOMATO PICKLES

green tomatoes
red peppers
dill
garlic cloves

1 quart vinegar
2 quarts water
1 cup pickling salt

Wash core and quarter green tomatoes. Pack them in sterile jars. Add 1 red pepper, 1 teaspoon dill and 1 garlic clove to each jar. Combine vinegar, water and pickling salt in a large sauce pan and bring to a boil. Pour this brine over tomatoes to fill jars within ½ inch of top. Seal the jars tightly with canning tops and turn upside down. After the seal is complete, store in a cool, dry place.

Note: You may need to prepare additional brine mixture according to the amount of tomatoes you are preparing.

Margaret Jenkins

PICKLED TOMATOES-CUCUMBERS

1 cup white vinegar
½ cup water
2 teaspoons sugar
¼ teaspoon salt

⅛ teaspoon pepper (½ pinch)
tomatoes
cucumbers

Mix the liquids with the sugar, salt and pepper in a refrigerator dish (covered). Wash and core tomatoes. (Don't peel). Cut into eighths or quarters, depending upon your preference of serving size. Put in the liquid. Peel and slice cucumbers into ⅛-¼ inch rounds. Put in the liquid. Ater 2-3 hours at room temperature, refrigerate until serving time. However, I do keep a dish in the refrigerator throughout the fresh vegetable season, adding the vegetables as needed. A new mixture is made up about each fortnight.

Shirley F. Burd

SQUASH RELISH

8 cups squash, chopped
2 cups onion, chopped
2 large bell peppers chopped
2 (4 ounce) cans pimiento,
   diced

3 cups sugar
2 cups white vinegar
1 teaspoon mustard seed

Drain vegetables one hour after chopping. Mix sugar, vinegar and mustard seed. Combine vegetables in a large pot and add sugar mixture. Bring to a boil and cook 5 minutes. Seal in sterlized jars.

Note: To vary the flavor you may want to add ½ teaspoon cinnamon and ½ teaspoon allspice.

L. Joye White

AUNT MAUCIE'S SWEET AND SOUR RELISH

5-6 ripe tomatoes, peeled and
   chopped
2 bell peppers, chopped fine
1 medium onion, chopped fine

⅛ cup sugar
½ cup vinegar
salt and pepper to taste

Combine all ingredients. Allow to marinate at least 2 hours.

Tine Keller

HORSERADISH

Horseradish roots (should equal about 2 cups)

2½ cups white vinegar
½ teaspoon salt

Wash the horseradish roots and peel off the brown outer skin. Cut into 1 inch pieces — at arm's length! Place in the blender with vinegar and salt. Grate using the appropriate setting on your blender. Store in an attractive jar in the refrigerator. Use aluminum foil in the lid if the top is not tightly sealed.

Note: For a special gift, wrap the jar in red cellophane and add a pretty ribbon.

Shirley F. Burd

SEASONING SALT

1 (26 ounce) box salt
2 tablespoons black pepper
3 tablespoons red pepper
3 tablespoons garlic powder

2 tablespoons chili powder
2 tablespoons monosodium glutamate

Combine all ingredients in a tightly sealed jar; mix well. This is an all-purpose seasoning and may be used on meats, vegetables, salads and fish.

Linden A. Webb

LOW CALORIE SOUR CREAM

1 cup dry curd cottage cheese
¼-½ cup buttermilk (depends on thickness desired)

¼ teaspoon lemon juice
pinch of salt

Combine ingredients in blender and mix until completely smooth. Refrigerate and serve. (This contains almost no fat and can be frozen). Does *not* withstand heat well.

Carolyn M. Oxford

III. Guidelines for Nutrition

Cheryl C. Stegbauer, Ed.

GUIDELINES FOR NUTRITION

Good nutrition is essential for preventing disease, promoting health, and for a feeling of well being. In the United States one rarely sees the results of severe nutritional deficiencies. Thus, "diet" often is thought of only as a treatment for a chronic disease or a health problem. However, the more subtle consequences of poor eating habits are found commonly. These include tooth decay, obesity (overweight), anemia in children, high blood pressure, and diabetes in adults. This section gives guidelines for healthy eating emphasizing disease prevention and nutrition during times of special need.

The Four Food Groups

Food nourishes the body and is essential for growth, maintenance, and repair. No single food group provides all of the materials required for a healthy body. Daily servings from each of the four food groups (bread/cereal, meat, milk, and vegetable/fruit) are necessary. This food plan adequately supplies protein, vitamins, and minerals. Examples of food sources for each of the four groups are:

1. Bread and Cereal Group: enriched or whole grain cereals, breads, biscuits, spaghetti, macaroni, noodles, hominy grits, crackers, cookies, cakes, rice, tapioca, flour.
2. Meat Group: meat (beef, pork, lamb, veal) fish, chicken, turkey, eggs, dried beans and peas, nuts, peanut butter.
3. Milk Group: milk (whole, skim, low fat, buttermilk, condensed, evaporated, dried), cheeses, ice cream.
4. Vegetable and Fruit Group: green leafy vegetables (lettuce, spinach, mustard, turnip greens, collards), yellow vegetables (carrots, sweet potatoes, squash, pumpkin), cabbage, broccoli, asparagus, citrus fruits (oranges, lemons, grapefruit), tomatoes, apples, bananas.

Good Food Habits

A selection of foods from the four food groups is a sound start for good nutrition. Additionally, the following food practices help avoid diet related health problems.

First, add fiber (roughage) to the diet. The typical diet in the United States is high in carbohydrates (sugars) and saturated fats (animal fats), and low in fiber. This diet causes problems with constipation and hemorrhoids. Also, there may be a connection between this eating pattern and other diseases such as colon cancer. High fiber is present in raw fruit and vegetables, whole grain breads, whole grain cereals, and whole grain rice (not "instant" rice).

Second, maintain a normal body weight. Obesity is associated with arthritis, gout, high blood pressure, heart disease, and diabetes in adults. Weight loss alone may lower blood sugar and blood pressure. Reducing or eliminating refined sugar intake and decreasing fats in the diet are good ways to reduce total calories.

Third, control the amount and type of fat eaten. Use polyunsaturated fats (vegetable fats) instead of saturated fats (animal fats). A diet low in saturated fats is recommended to prevent certain types of heart disease. Replace animal fats with corn oil, safflower oil, soybean oil, or peanut oil. Trim visible fat from meats. Use low fat or skim milk, and substitute plain low-fat yogurt for sour cream to reduce fats and calories. Egg yolk is high in cholesterol (a saturated fat), but egg white contains almost no fat. Substitute two egg whites for one whole egg without changing the end result of most recipes.

Fourth, eliminate or eat less sugar. The calories from sugar are "empty" calories and have no food value. Refined sugar contributes to obesity and tooth decay. In some individuals, refined sugars in the diet contribute to a high blood level of triglycerides (a form of fat).

Fifth, use as little salt (sodium) as possible. A high salt intake leads to hypertension in some individuals. Anyone with a family history or high blood pressure should avoid salt. After decreasing salt intake, many become better able to taste salt. Thus, less salt is required. Common high salt foods are cured or canned meats, cold cuts, salted snacks (chips, crackers, pickles), catsup, seasoned salts (garlic, celery, onion), baking soda, baking powder, canned soups, "diet" colas, and frozen processed foods (fish fillets). Be creative in cooking. Instead of salt, flavor with garlic, lemon, onion, or vinegar. Additional herbs and spices are listed below:

Herbs and Spices for Vegetables

CABBAGE	Thyme, marjoram, basil
GREENS (Turnips, collard, mustard, spinach)	Bay leaf, marjoram, thyme
GREEN BEANS	Thyme, bay leaf, sugar, lemon juice
POTATOES	Nutmeg, parsley, ginger, marjoram, thyme
SQUASH	Allspice, sage, ginger, vinegar

Herbs and Spices for Meats

BEEF	Basil, marjoram, thyme, green pepper, onion, pepper
CHICKEN	Chili powder, oregano, basil, sage, thyme, lemon juice
FISH	Ginger, nutmeg, oregano, sage, lemon juice
PORK	Basil, marjoram, sage, onion

Times of Special Nutritional Need

Infancy: 1-12 months

Infancy is the most critical time in a child's nutritional life. One of a variety of diet plans may supply the infant's food requirements as long as some general guidelines are followed.

The American Academy of Pediatrics recommends that infants remain on breast milk or iron fortified formula through the first year of life. Skim milk, lowfat milk, and whole cow's milk are not recommended during the first year of life. Baby foods (semi-solids) are unnecessary during the first 6 months of life. Before 6 months, the infant's digestive and neurological systems are immature. Also, some authorities think that early food consumption during infancy may lead to obesity and development of allergies. The use of a syringe-like device to force feed an immature infant is undesirable. When the infant is able to participate in feeding, baby foods can begin. Signs of readiness include sitting without support and good head control.

When introducing baby foods, begin with rice cereal. This is least likely to cause an allergic reaction. Next, try vegetables, then fruits, and last meats. Consider fruit juices a fruit. Of the juices, add orange juice last, since allergy to it is common. Also, for the same reason, do not give eggs until nine months of age. Introduce new foods one at a time and one month apart. This allows observation for reactions to a new food. Read labels to select baby foods without added salt, sugar, tapioca, or cornstarch. Be aware that "mixed dinners" are expensive and contain little meat. Also, "high protein dinners" contain only ½ the protein of pure meats.

Feeding is one of the infant's first pleasant experiences. When the need for food is promptly met the infant learns to trust. Infants need to be held during feedings with the atmosphere as calm as possible. Parents often show concern about whether an infant is getting enough food. A steady gain in weight and length is a good indication of adequate diet.

Toddlerhood: 1-3 years

Toddlerhood is a challenging developmental period. Continuing maturation of motor skills makes self-feeding possible. Encouragement and praise are important as these new skills develop.

Normal behaviors can be trying or disturbing to parents. Toddlers may be particular about food preparation and service. The child may demand a specific plate or cup and may refuse food not prepared a certain way. The child's appetite decreases because of a slowed growth rate. Thus, the child is a "picky" eater. Weaning from the bottle becomes important to ensure an adequate intake of solids and to prevent tooth decay. It is important to avoid nagging or forcing children to eat unwanted food. It is helpful to recognize that these food habits are temporary. Also, the type of food eaten is more important than amount. When only nutritious foods and snacks are available, the child likely will receive a well balanced diet. Most younger children need to eat between meals because of their small stomachs and sporadic appetites. Good snacks to encourage are hard-boiled eggs, fruits, raw vegetables, and peanut butter with cracker (for older toddlers). For a child who does not like milk, substitutes include cottage cheese, vanilla ice cream, or American cheese.

The emotional environment at mealtime may influence food intake. The atmosphere at the dinner table should be pleasant. Making conversation with the child during meals reinforces appropriate eating behavior and increases food intake.

The Preschooler: 4-6 years

Few children pass through the pre-school years without creating concern regarding their food intake. Appetites are usually unpredictable during this period. Pre-schoolers become less interested in food and more interested in their environment. Few pre-school age children conform to a three meal a day pattern. A child may eat two well-balanced meals and several nutritious snacks throughout the day and not require a third meal. Food fads are common, and likes and dislikes may change from day to day. It is wise to offer new foods frequently, even if previously refused. Also, new settings provide exposure to many foods. Day care centers, kindergartens, and pre-schools can be a source for learning good food habits.

School Age: 7-10 years

The school age period is one of steady growth accompanied by few feeding problems. Good nutrition is vital in this period because undernourished children become easily fatigued and unable to sustain the physical and mental effort necessary for learning.

Breakfast is an important meal, since mid-morning snacks are not available in most schools. Many cereals contain large amounts of sugar and have little nutritional value. Fresh fruit or juice, milk, and peanut butter on whole wheat toast provide a quick but nutritious breakfast. Fruit and cheese are nutritious after school snacks.

The knowledge of nutrition and attitudes acquired during this period provide a basis for the years when the decisions of food selection become the child's own. Children readily adopt the family attitudes toward food and eating. However, some school age children express their individuality through food preferences. If the total intake is sufficient in basic content, it generally is wise to yield to these fads rather than nag, persuade or discipline.

Adolescence: 11-20 years

Adolescence is a period of rapid physical growth with increased requirements for calories and nutritious foods. Getting the proper food may be difficult for the adolescent because of several factors. These include: 1) a desire to express a developing sense of self and independence by following extreme "diets," 2) an inability to grasp the effect of present food intake on future health, and 3) insufficient time to prepare or eat nutritious foods.

The adolescent's diet most often is lacking in iron, calcium, and vitamins A, C, and D. This is corrected by a daily intake of 3 glasses of milk, one serving of a green leafy vegetable, one glass of citrus juice, and 2 servings from the meat group. The "fast foods," common in an adolescent's diet, can provide a balanced meal if selected foods are added. A carton of milk and a piece of fruit teamed with a hamburger is a nutritious meal for a teenager. Pizza and tacos, although high in sodium (salt) and calories, are good choices of fast foods.

Adolescents tend to eat whatever is convenient. Thus, nutritious snack foods should be easily available. Suggested snacks are fresh fruits and juices, cheese, fresh vegetables (carrot sticks, celery sticks), milk, nuts, jello with fruit, peanut butter on crackers, puddings, and oatmeal cookies with raisins or nuts.

Certain adolescents require individualized food planning. They are the athelete, the pregnant or breast feeding female, and the adolescent with emotional problems affecting eating behavior and diet.

Pregnancy

What should a prospective mother know about nutrition in pregnancy? First, weight gain is important. The size of the baby relates to the mother's weight before pregnancy as well as her weight gain during pregnancy. A woman who is at her ideal weight before pregnancy (using a standard height weight table) should gain approximately 25 pounds. An underweight woman should gain the amount she is underweight plus 25 pounds. The theory that thin is beautiful is not true in pregnancy. The overweight woman should not diet. She should attempt to gain 25 pounds. Poor food habits such as dieting or skipping meals may be harmful.

Second, the rate of weight gain is also important. A baby grows the most in the last three months of pregnancy. Therefore, a woman at or near her ideal weight should gain approximately 10 pounds by the end of the fifth month. She should gain ¾ to one pound a week from the fifth month until she gives birth. If a woman gains too quickly she should attempt to slow her weight gain. She should not stop gaining.

Third, "junk food" is not recommended. A healthy mother can salt her food to taste, but she should avoid poor snacks such as salty chips. She should be certain to include every day:

4 servings from the milk group;
4 servings of fruits and vegetables;
6-9 ounces of meat; and,
4 or more servings of breads and cereals depending on her weight gain and the calories needed to gain at the optimum rate.

Breast feeding

Breast feeding requires even more energy than pregnancy. Also, the amount of milk produced daily depends on the mother's state of nutrition. A well-nourished mother requires about 500 additional calories per day for adequate milk production. These extra calories do not add to the mother's body fat.

A diet lacking in vitamins results in breast milk with these same deficiencies. In addition to daily servings from the four food groups, the mother needs extra vitamin C, folic acid, vitamin E, and protein. A fresh orange provides the additional vitamin C and folic acid. Wheat germ or a few tablespoons of margarine or salad dressing supplies vitamin E. A quart of milk each day plus an extra serving from the meat group provide ample protein.

Maturity and Older Age

Calcium often is lacking in the diets of the elderly. Also, there may be a deficiency in iron, thiamine and riboflavin. A diet including foods from the milk group, dried peas or beans, and red meat, should avoid these common deficiencies. The elderly at greatest risk for malnutrition are at the poverty level, chronically ill, live alone or are over 75 years.

The following suggestions are helpful for problems common to the elderly.

1. Be aware of the amounts of salt and sugar added to foods. With aging comes a decrease in the ability to taste, leading to use of additional sugar and salt.
2. Foods such as fruits and vegetables provide roughage in the diet and prevent constipation.
3. Drink at least six or seven glasses of fluid a day. This also helps prevent constipation and supplies the body with needed water.
4. Poor teeth or poorly fitting dentures make chewing difficult. Practice good oral hygiene.
5. Share meals when possible. This helps stimulate the appetite and may be less costly.
6. Ask your doctor or nurse about the affect of medicines on nutrition. For example, mineral oil can keep the body from using certain vitamins.
7. Eat only when sitting. This makes swallowing easier and helps prevent choking.
8. Help with meals or advice about foods is available from the local Dietetic Association, Senior Citizens Groups, the Department of Agriculture, Public Health Department and local Homemaker Services.

Index

Index

An Apple A Day: TNA District #1
Post Office Box 40801
Memphis,TN 38104-0801

Please send me _____ copies of An Apple A Day at $10.95 plus $1.55
handling. TN residents add 6% sales tax.
Enclosed is my check or money order for $_____

Name_____

Address_____

City_____State_____Zip_____

An Apple A Day: TNA District #1
Post Office Box 40801
Memphis,TN 38104-0801

Please send me _____ copies of An Apple A Day at $10.95 plus $1.55
handling. TN residents add 6% sales tax.
Enclosed is my check or money order for $_____

Name_____

Address_____

City_____State_____Zip_____

An Apple A Day: TNA District #1
Post Office Box 40801
Memphis,TN 38104-0801

Please send me _____ copies of An Apple A Day at $10.95 plus $1.55
handling. TN residents add 6% sales tax.
Enclosed is my check or money order for $_____

Name_____

Address_____

City_____State_____Zip_____

An Apple A Day: TNA District #1
Post Office Box 40801
Memphis,TN 38104-0801

Please send me _____ copies of An Apple A Day at $10.95 plus $1.55
handling. TN residents add 6% sales tax.
Enclosed is my check or money order for $_____

Name_____

Address_____

City_____State_____Zip_____

- -

An Apple A Day: TNA District #1
Post Office Box 40801
Memphis,TN 38104-0801

Please send me _____ copies of An Apple A Day at $10.95 plus $1.55
handling. TN residents add 6% sales tax.
Enclosed is my check or money order for $_____

Name_____

Address_____

City_____State_____Zip_____

- -

An Apple A Day: TNA District #1
Post Office Box 40801
Memphis,TN 38104-0801

Please send me _____ copies of An Apple A Day at $10.95 plus $1.55
handling. TN residents add 6% sales tax.
Enclosed is my check or money order for $_____

Name_____

Address_____

City_____State_____Zip_____

Re-OrderAdditionalCopies